COMMANDING REVERENCE

A JOURNEY TO RECLAIM RELEVANCE AND REVERENCE OF THE TEN COMMANDMENTS

LIBBY PENDERGAST

Jennifer ~

Remember the Sabbath,
abiding in him for joy, peace
and abundance!   *Libby ♡*

LifeRich
PUBLISHING®

Matthew 22:37

LifeRich Publishing is a registered trademark of The Reader's Digest Association, Inc.

LifeRich Publishing books may be ordered through booksellers or by contacting:

LifeRich Publishing
1663 Liberty Drive
Bloomington, IN 47403
www.liferichpublishing.com
844-686-9607

Because of the dynamic nature of the Internet, any web addresses or links contained in this book may have changed since publication and may no longer be valid. The views expressed in this work are solely those of the author and do not necessarily reflect the views of the publisher, and the publisher hereby disclaims any responsibility for them.

Cover painting by Donna Riley Hearne used with permission.

Author photo by Ellie French used with permission.

Any people depicted in stock imagery provided by Getty Images are models, and such images are being used for illustrative purposes only. Certain stock imagery © Getty Images.

Scripture quotations are from the ESV® Bible (The Holy Bible, English Standard Version®), Copyright © 2001 by Crossway, a publishing ministry of Good News Publishers. Used by permission. All rights reserved.

ISBN: 978-1-4897-4446-3 (sc)
ISBN: 978-1-4897-4445-6 (hc)
ISBN: 978-1-4897-4444-9 (e)

Library of Congress Control Number: 2022918172

Print information available on the last page.

LifeRich Publishing rev. date: 11/22/2022

DEDICATION

I dedicate this book to my dear family and friends—the
precious warriors who share life with me, love me, and
bring me joy just by being who they are each day:

Specifically, my mother, who molded me and taught
me about God, His unconditional love, and hers;
My husband, who loves, supports, and encourages
me every day to be who God calls me to be;
My children, whom I love beyond measure—their hearts
beat with mine and they fill my cup every day;
My family and dear friends who have prayed for
me and cheered me on along this journey;
May God shine His light on you all and pour
His abundance over you all your days!

CONTENTS

Preface 9

Acknowledgments 11

Introduction 13

Chapter 1   God's Guardrails 15
Chapter 2   Myths and Consequences 33
Chapter 3   Self-Righteous Checklist...................51
Chapter 4   Religious Buffet 71
Chapter 5   Risky Business 89
Chapter 6   Wise Old Owls 109
Chapter 7   What We Worship............................131
Chapter 8   Love...151

Summing It Up … 171
Advice from My Children and Mentors...............175
Perspective … 177
About the Cover...179
Playlist Inspiring Me Along This Journey 183
Notes 185

PREFACE

Now therefore go and I will be with your mouth
and teach you what you shall speak.

—Exodus 4:12

Writing a book was a mere idea in the back of my mind for over a decade. I was intrigued with the thought, and then it left me altogether for a time. Then, one summer day several years later, while in my mother's northern Michigan home, I clearly heard the Lord say to me, "Use your voice." I didn't fully understand it. Although I clearly heard the words and even wrote them down at the time, I questioned what He meant. I questioned if it was in fact God that I heard. What was this feeling in my spirit that continued nudging me, and how was I to use my voice? His words continued to repeat in my mind for months, finally leading me on a quest to understand my calling.

I began unwinding notes I had collected, believing I knew the subject of my book. That distinctly changed months later when my subject shifted to what was unmistakably the Lord telling me I was going to write a completely different book. I listened, became obedient and have now written a book about the Ten Commandments.

It's important to share the message of how I came to be an author. There's no question this book is inspired by the Lord for His purposes. His will for me to write excited me to share the importance of listening to God's voice and leaning into our gifts and His call for us. I didn't want to debate with God on why He wanted me to write about the Ten Commandments. I just knew He asked me to write about them, and I intended to do as He asked with faith He would guide me along the way. I wasn't certain how He would use my writing experience and the book for His glory. All I knew was that I trusted God in this process and was determined to see it through. What abundance I feel from obedience!

ACKNOWLEDGMENTS

Special thanks to my children, Dawson, Walker, and Ellie French; to Joye Cook, Tim Land, Nick Strobel, and my stepfather Reverend Dr. Jim McLean for allowing me to interview them for their perspectives on the Ten Commandments, and to my brother Randy Becker, Tina Myers, Tim, and Nick as members of a focus group providing me with biblical reader insight from my first draft to book completion. All of their input was extremely valuable and filled with many nuggets of wisdom.

My church small group for continued prayer during this journey. They are all warriors!

Scot Longyear, senior pastor at Maryland Community Church, Terre Haute, for countless inspiring sermons and generous guidance on becoming a published author.

My darling cousins Amelia Hearne, Evie Revel and Kit Wilkinson for their creative insights, talents and enthusiasm towards assisting me in cover design and collateral imagery. Lastly, a special acknowledgment of their grandmother, my late cousin Donna Hearne; She inspired me to be bold in the truth and a woman of action, participating in life with conviction.

INTRODUCTION

Oh how I love your law!
It is my meditation all the day.
Your commandment makes me wiser than my
enemies, for it is ever with me.

—Psalm 119:97–98

We have all broken all of the Ten Commandments; yes all of us, all of them. You may be thinking that isn't true; you've not committed adultery, used the name of the Lord in vain, or committed murder. Or have you? After rediscovering the Ten Commandments, I realized that not only had I broken some of the commandments—I had broken all ten. The good news is that having broken them, I later understood how better to follow them. Through my breaking them, God helped me understand how much I still need them. We all need them for joy and abundance, so why do we often forget their relevance and reverence in our daily lives? Becoming obedient to His commandments led me to peace, joy, and an abundant life and will do the same for you.

I invite you into a conversation with me as we journey through the relevance, mysteries, and reverence of the Ten Commandments. I share some of my personal stories and how God used my life challenges, occasionally prideful yet honest nature, and curious observations to draw closer to Him. I ask questions for all of us to consider and give you space to answer them after each chapter. My book offers an opportunity of discovery for each of us to love our Father more deeply and grow in our personal paths of obedience to Him—not only by abiding in the Ten Commandments but in using our gifts for His glory.

Please join me in exploring the Ten Commandments in a new way, and prepare for the Holy Spirit to speak to you, too. I am confident that our heavenly Father has blessed what is written. In many parts of the book, I can say with assurance that the words on the page were not written by me, but I was the chosen scribe for what God wanted to be said. I wrote this book for a purpose, and as of print, I'm not clear of the full purpose, but I do believe He asked me to write it, and I'm grateful you have chosen to read it.

Because there are Ten Commandments you'll likely expect ten chapters. There are eight. Don't ask me why; just know that I write about the Ten Commandments in an unexpected, nonsequential way. For those orderly readers, just roll with it, and I promise it will make sense in the end. Although not a theologian, I'm a student of God's Word and have formed insight and perspective from a myriad of sources, most notably the Holy Spirit and the Holy Bible. All of these resources from scripture to my mentors and scholars have contributed to this surprising experience eagerly awaiting you.

God gave us the Ten Commandments as guardrails to protect us and bring us joy. My hope is you will find my book relatable, honest, and useful as a tool in building a stronger relationship with the Lord. Perhaps you will view the Ten Commandments through a new lens and consider a new point of view. I pray you're inspired to find abundance by being obedient to God's Ten Commandments and His call for your purpose.

> Delight yourself in the Lord, and he will give you the desires of your heart.
> —Psalm 37:4

ONE
GOD'S GUARDRAILS

You shall walk in all the way that the Lord your
God has commanded you, that you may live, and
that it may go well with you, and that you may
live long in the land that you shall possess.
                                    —Deuteronomy 5:33

For years when I thought about the Ten Commandments, two
memories always came to mind. One was of me, nervously
standing in front of our minister in his office at Christ Episcopal
Church, Little Rock. I was like all the other sixth graders preparing
for confirmation (my public affirmation of faith recommitting
baptism). It was now my turn to recite the Ten Commandments
from memory in order to complete my confirmation requirements
and successfully pass. To this day I can see my twelve-year-old self
worried that I would miss a word or worse, blank on one of the
Commandments. I had a strong short-term memory, so it worked
out in my favor to recall them for the test. However, over time
they became easier to skew and forget.

Easy to forget, until the time of year when I was reminded
of them again; enter my second vivid memory of the Ten
Commandments. Actor Charlton Heston and the highly acclaimed
movie *The Ten Commandments* should receive dual credit for my
remembering them. Who can forget the dramatic scene of Moses
standing, overcome and exhilarated from just speaking with God
as the Commandments were spoken to him? Charlton Heston,

playing Moses, cued my memory of the important rules God had written for us through this nugget of cinema, His commands to His people portrayed on the big screen; there was Moses, wind in his hair, clouds swirling on a mountaintop, holding the sacred two tablets over his head while the light of God shone down on him. This had an impact on me year after year. The Academy Award–winning movie aired on our local channel reminding us of all the grandeur of the Ten Commandments.

In my young mind, I knew they mattered, and I knew they were important, but there seemed to be a disconnect between hearing of them a little and living them out a lot. Why did they matter? Were they relevant? Understood? We knew God wrote them in the Old Testament, so did they still apply in the New Testament? All these years later, thousands actually, it seems to me that many of the same questions could be asked. Misunderstanding them or questioning their full relevance are just a couple of questions that come to mind, particularly when observing how society can disregard them as sacred, if regarding them at all.

When I began writing, the Holy Spirit led me to interview my children and a few of my mentors for content. What I found interesting is that, whatever their age or theological knowledge of the Bible, they all paused to recite all Ten Commandments ... accurately. There are only ten, and many of us have known of them more than fifty years, so why are they hard to remember? Why can't some of us remember them all? Are they still relevant? What happened to the Ten Commandments?

These are some of the many questions I started contemplating a few years ago. I started to notice when people would gossip, and then in the next breath they were swearing, but through it all they called themselves Christians. I began processing a disconnect between my observations and what my biblical foundation taught me. My guardrails for truth were now in question, so I started paying more attention to these behaviors, particularly my own.

By now you may be asking yourself, what are the Ten Commandments again? Do you remember them all? Have you already put the book down to look them up and confirm how many you knew or even started going down the list to see how many you've not broken, or maybe just sort of broken, or broken a long time ago? Justification and negotiating thoughts may be kicking in; by nature we all want to get it right, pass the test, make the cut, win the prize, pass go, and, most importantly, go to heaven! Do the Ten Commandments help us get us there? If yes how? If not, then why should we care whether we follow them? I don't suggest we depend on our own righteousness for salvation but have faith in Christ's righteousness. So how are the Ten Commandments still relevant in our modern world?

The Ten Commandments are spoken specifically in Exodus and then again in Deuteronomy. God, His prophets, and His disciples talk about them many more times throughout both the Old and New Testaments of the Bible in multiple ways. To me this deems them important. I wonder why did He write them? Why did He choose the specific time to write them, and why is it important that we follow them? On this journey, possible answers will be revealed and possibly more questions evolve. My prayer is for you to experience both. With more questions of the Ten Commandments may come more understanding and perspective!

1. I am the Lord thy God; You shall have no other gods before me.
2. You shall not make for yourself carved images...
3. You shall not take the name of the Lord your God in vain.
4. Remember the Sabbath day, to keep it holy.

5. Honor your father and your mother, that your days may be long in the land the Lord your God is giving you.
6. You shall not murder.
7. You shall not commit adultery
8. You shall not steal
9. You shall not bear false witness against your neighbor.
10. You shall not covet... (Exodus 20:2–4, 7–8, 12–17)

Where's "love your neighbor as yourself?" My daughter Ellie thinks of this as one of the Ten Commandments, and she wouldn't be wrong. So did it not make the original top ten? "Love your neighbor as yourself" is the second greatest commandment.

"Teacher, which is the greatest commandment in the law?"

> Jesus replied: "Love the Lord your God with all your heart and with all your soul and with all your mind.' This is the first and greatest commandment. And the second is like it: 'Love your neighbor as yourself.' All the Law and the Prophets hang on these two commandments." (Matthew 22:36–40)

That makes it all clear right? Yes, if we look at the words Jesus spoke to place emphasis on two things: love God and love people. If we do this, we are following God's Ten Commandments.

According to some historians, there was an adaptive difference in the commandments for different religions. Basically religious Jews, Catholics, Protestants, and Greek Orthodox all believe the same commandments, but they're worded a bit differently and in varying orders. That said, it would be easier and much clearer if they were literally all the same. Still, what is abundantly clear and the same in all translations is that we are to *love God* and *love people.*

How do we get to this place of relationship to God and His people? It's been an incredible experience to watch my own life evolving from a place of fear, anxiety, control, and classic commandment negotiator in life's circumstances to the peace and joy of truly knowing God's commandments. Aiming to abide by them each day has opened my heart and mind in wonderful ways. Trying to live my life anew in Christ by following God's law every day, not just on Sundays or when I'm around certain people, has offered the freedom, joy, and abundance I once thought ironically I would lose if I followed the Ten Commandments. A growing awareness of listening to the Lord and feeling the Holy Spirit working inside me has caused an awakening. This nudging me to wake up, be bold, pay attention, and not simply accept the hypocrisy all around me in the world has stirred my emotions. The goal is trying to understand the Ten Commandments with more clarity and intentionality.

If I'm having these observations, it occurred to me that perhaps I'm not alone. Maybe you've noticed this too. For instance, are the Commandments misunderstood? I asked my son Dawson if he believed the Ten Commandments were misunderstood, and he thought they weren't actually understood to begin with. Keen observation! If they aren't understood enough, then that could mean a couple of things. One, as a society we have forgotten that the Ten Commandments are God's guardrails to protect us and keep us from veering off course. He created them for us to know peace, joy, and abundance,, and practically speaking, they are truly guardrails for us to have a framework of right and wrong and not cross the line without a consequence. Shouldn't we have awareness of the "rules" so we can decide if we are willing to break them? How do we know murder is wrong? Who made the law or rule that stealing is bad and has consequences? I'm not sure how often we sit around wondering these things, and if we lack awareness of the foundation for these and the other eight commandments, where is our consciousness?

People who say they love God likely have much more understanding of the Ten Commandments, but a question to ask our naysayer friends and fellow sin negotiators is why would God give His people the Ten Commandments; for what purpose? There may be more than one purpose. Ask yourself, what if I have misunderstood the Ten Commandments, and if I have, what have I possibly misunderstood?—and not just from the church or religious perspective.

Consider that many cultures and countries have established rules of law, pillars of conduct, and fundamental frameworks from the original Ten Commandments. I hadn't considered any of this until I started interviewing a couple of my more biblically educated mentors. My discovery turned out to be obvious and yet nothing I had thought about before. When we learn the history of countries around the world and of our own United States of America, it's exciting to conceive how the framers of our nation relied on God and His commandments to establish the foundations for our society.

An example of this precise point was published in a paper written by William J Federer in 2001. He referenced several quotes by our second United States president, John Adams. "The Ten Commandments and the Sermon on the Mount contain my religion," Adams wrote to Thomas Jefferson on November 4, 1816. This is significant, from a signer of our Declaration of Independence.

Further examination of over 15,000 documents, from pamphlets to newspaper articles to books written between 1760 and 1805 by the fifty-five men who wrote the Constitution, revealed that 34 percent of the quotes from our founding fathers were from the Bible; Deuteronomy in particular. The quote that moved me the most was from John Adam's diary entry February 22, 1756:

> Suppose a nation in some distant Region should take the Bible for their only law Book, and every member should regulate his conduct by the precepts there exhibited! Every member would be obliged in conscience, to temperance, frugality, and industry; to justice, kindness, and charity towards his fellow men; and to piety, love, and reverence toward Almighty God … What a Eutopia, what a Paradise would this region be.

The reverence for God that our founding fathers presented was then and is now sobering. The Ten Commandments meant something grander to model a right society. If we fast-forward 250 years, we can still see this reverence engraved on many significant structures across our land. I challenge you to do a little research on this and scout them out the next time you're in a city hall, university, or one of our nation's courthouses. At one time and as far as I am aware, still, you will find the Supreme Court building architecture hosts a sculpture of the Ten Commandments with Moses holding the two tablets. They were also engraved over the chair of the Chief Justice and on the bronze doors of the Supreme Court. This is quite significant when you think about it. Why would the Ten Commandments be lauded in this way? Is it because they inspired the laws of our nation? There are countless places where the Ten Commandments have been placed right in front of our eyes, but how often have we noticed?

Is it because they're taken for granted, largely misunderstood, or not understood enough? Or as my stepfather, the ever-clever Fr

Jim McLean, said to me, "Oh yes, they're understood, but many people don't believe they're relevant to their lives. They know what they say, but people don't really consider them so much as they walk through their daily lives." ... Scary, but true?

I wonder why we push the boundaries where the Ten Commandments are concerned. Once I started asking this question of a few more friends and family, I was intrigued with the responses. Dawson's perspective drives the point home that because the Ten Commandments aren't fully understood to begin with, there's no real understanding of what they mean even if you could recite the list. Without understanding, how do you know that you're not following them? Whether a long-time follower of Christ or new to the faith, I believe we've all struggled to comprehend their truest value. How beautiful they are, and what a gift we have available for knowing abundance and joy. The trick is figuring this out by being obedient to them. The funny thing is that breaking the commandments ultimately led me to honoring them.

As the American motion picture producer and director Cecil B DeMille stated at the 1956 premiere of *The Ten Commandments* film,

> The Ten Commandments are not the laws. They are *THE LAW.* Man has made 32 million laws since the Commandments were handed down to Moses on Mount Sinai more than three thousand years ago, but he has never improved on God's law. The Ten Commandments are the principles by which man may live with God and man may live with man. They are the expressions of the mind of God for His creatures. They are the

charter and guide of human liberty, for there can
be no liberty without the law.

He went on to say that he hoped people would walk away
from the film:

> Filled with the spirit of truth. That it will bring
> to its audience a better understanding of the real
> meaning of this pattern of life that God has set
> down for us to follow.

As God's children, we have been given the absolute playbook
for protection and abundance. Have we become overwhelmed with
all the "rules" to follow? This is possibly one point of confusion
in true understanding of the commandments. By looking at the
commandments as guardrails rather than rules, maybe we will see
how they aren't there to keep us from joy but quite the opposite.
Ultimately, I don't believe most of us look to break them, although
we all have and still do. Forgiveness from God is a foregone
conclusion for some who ask, "Does the sin I commit matter?"
I say yes it does. Throwing up our hands to continue trying to
follow them isn't the answer. The question we all ask is do they
still matter for us to follow and why? Does it matter to God, and
does what He thinks of me matter?

I have to admit that when I was younger, I honestly wasn't
sure what to think about God. I knew I wanted to love Him, and
I believed what I was told, that he loved me—especially because
I was a child, and I heard God loves all the little children. So why
was I a little bit afraid of Him? Was it because I feared Him in the
actual scary way? Was it because I didn't want to make a mistake
or disappoint God? Was it because I didn't fully understand what
He was asking me when He said to remember the Sabbath or not
to covet? Most likely all of the answers are yes. I didn't fully get it

and was too embarrassed to ask questions. What if I was the only one in Sunday school who had these questions? Would everyone laugh at me? I adapted the ever reliable "fake it till you make it" mentality. Until one day when I watched what became one of my favorite movies, *Fiddler on the Roof,* and I had an epiphany about one of the Ten Commandments.

Who would have thought that Tevye and his wife Golde contributed to enlightening me as to what the Sabbath was all about? I was fascinated watching Golde prepare the Sabbath table and fuss over everyone's attendance. The dots were connecting, and seeing the sanctity in the ceremony, the prayers, family, respect, and honor taking priority over all else made an impact on me. This is when it came together in my spirit for the first time how important this commandment was to understand, but there were still many questions. How did the Jewish doctrine make sense for me, as a Christian? Is it still necessary to regard the Sabbath Day, and why is it important enough that God commanded us to remember it and keep it holy? "So then, there remains a Sabbath rest for the people of God, for whoever has entered God's rest has also rested from his works as God did from his. Let us therefore strive to enter that rest, so that no one may fall by the same sort of disobedience" (Hebrews 4:9–11).

I can't recall ever hearing a sermon about the Sabbath. I was likely in the congregation more than once for an excellent sermon on the subject, but none are coming to mind—not because they weren't well written or well executed, but because I can't recall ever listening to one with intent. If I did hear a sermon about the Sabbath, it didn't stick, at least not enough to convict my heart to honor or remember it. I'm still challenged to remember the Sabbath with intent. Why is this difficult to do? I wonder if it has anything to do with tradition. What would Tevye say?

As I grew up in Little Rock, tradition was always going to

church on Sundays. Dressing up in our finest, we would arrive early and on our lucky days, we got there in time to snag one of the remaining pieces of yummy toast left over from the early breakfast crowd. We would run around the church and find all the nooks and crannies in fascination; then we would meet our parents in the church sanctuary. After church, we took a scenic drive home, where we had a simple lunch. Then it was common to call on our elder relatives. This tradition was beautiful in my eyes, and although there were days when my brother Randy and I protested the visits, we always had a nice time listening to the stories of the past and spending time together.

Another family tradition was on Sunday evenings. We would often order Kentucky Fried Chicken and eat that delicious bucket of decadence while watching the *Wonderful World of Disney*. This was a highlight and treat for our family—and frankly a big deal to have a restaurant open on a Sunday to cater to our taste buds. Sometime in the late seventies, it seems more and more places of business started opening on Sundays. It was a faint conversation by most and a toss-up of reactions between appalled at the gall to be open on a Sunday and secretly gleeful to take full advantage of all the options now available on Sundays. From restaurants to grocery stores, hardware stores, and the mother ship—the mall— all were going to start opening, but only from one to five o'clock, so we could all go to church first before we indulged in all the newfound conveniences.

Looking back, we combined family time with having a servant's heart and sacred God time on Sundays. God is our family, and the tradition of spending the day with Him was expected and joyful. Have we veered away from the sanctity of hardly anything open on Sundays and the given that Sundays were for family, rest, God, the Sabbath, to the mass blurred lines of when and even if there is a Sabbath to remember? Have we caved to pressure in our culture of doing more? And here's another question: is the Sabbath on Sunday, or is it on Saturday? What time does it begin, and when does it end? Depending on your faith, your religion, or, as my friend Pastor Nick Strobel so eloquently puts it, "your soup of reality," can it be any day you pick? I love that expression, soup of reality. Just add what you need to satisfy your palate, mix, and consume.

Can we decide each week what day works for us to acknowledge the Sabbath? I've had friends tell me yes, you can, as long as you are truly devoting one day a week to purposefully reflect and focus on God. I guess whether these details matter truly does depend on our faith or religion. I can honestly admit that for most of my life I hadn't "Remembered the Sabbath" at least not consistently. In the back of mind and in my spirit I did sense I needed and wanted to, yet I didn't commit to it. Since reacquainting myself with the Ten Commandments, it's been more on my heart to seek peace on Sundays and enjoy the day focusing on the Lord and my family, just like the commandment asks us to do and just like the tradition of my childhood.

What should be one of the easiest commandments to keep and one we would most want to keep—rest, do nothing, chill, and replenish—apparently can be a real struggle! Why don't we want to rest or, better yet, take a complimentary vacation day each week? Give ourselves permission to not be busy, take a nap, read a book, take a walk, breathe in nature, and, most importantly, sit back, be still, and give thanks to God for His creation and *all* He has done and will do for us? The Sabbath is a gift God gave us so that we can be restored. God took a day of rest after creating the universe; don't we need a rest too? If we don't honor the Sabbath, are we saying we're better than God and don't need the rest? "And on the seventh day God finished his work which he had done, and he rested on the seventh day from all his work which he had done" Genesis 2:2.

Where it gets murky for me is the reality we live in now. Many people would struggle, primarily financially, if they didn't work extra jobs, catch up on chores, and prepare for the week ahead. Can these believers be given a Sabbath pass? There's got to be a loophole in the Ten Commandments for extenuating circumstances. Would God understand this as a gray area, since when He wrote the Ten Commandments, some of today's life demands didn't exist? Some are more serious demands than others, but nonetheless they exist, including soccer leagues on the Sabbath and football! That's not really a distraction though, is it? Being together as a family is what's important on this day, so how is this a problem?

We get distracted from remembering! That is God's point, I believe: to ask us, His children, to take pause for a day and remember to keep it holy. In other words, dedicate a day to focus on God, be centered in Him, rest and replenish our souls, and strengthen our relationship with Him. It sounds so easy and doable, but if you're like me, this isn't necessarily easy at all.

I have to commend the people who don't have this sin struggle. I recognize the businesses with the courage to stand up to public pressure, honoring their personal core values rather than operating for the status quo. When the world clashes with what God is asking, who has the strength not to buckle to the pressures of the world? Chick-fil-A and Hobby Lobby are two companies that have succeeded in maintaining their convictions. We notice and accept it, and I personally admire them for it. In addition to respecting their values, by holding the line, honoring God, and encouraging their employees and customers to do the same, they're acknowledging God's guardrails and modeling the need for us to do the same. These businesses are doing their part to advance the kingdom.

What am I doing to advance His kingdom on the Sabbath? Do I model what God is asking me to do? Did I model to my children when they were required to participate in sports on a Sunday that it wasn't a big deal to do so? It was a challenge in our family back then because the world is saying, "If you don't show up for practice or a game instead of going to church, there might be consequences." The question then becomes, what consequences might we suffer if we don't obey what the Lord is asking? "Remember the Sabbath" is a commandment. God wrote it for a reason as one of our guardrails—I believe, to help us stay close to Him. If we practice remembering the Sabbath, we will be less likely to get distracted.

There were definitely times when raising our children it was difficult to stand firm in our convictions. Putting God first, then our family, and time pouring into one another was something to strive for, and having our children in church, building their spiritual foundations, was of paramount importance to me.

Ellie and I recently reminisced about her memories of a typical childhood Sunday. It was so delightful hearing how our often-hurried Sunday mornings and unscheduled afternoons etched deep memories for her. Reflecting back, she sees images of us getting dressed up in our nice clothes and attending church, followed by going out for family lunch. They were happy, meaningful days to her, especially in the smallest ways. They felt like reset days. Relaxing coupled with some fun and maybe an errand or two. Sunday was an important day and Ellie acknowledged it as a sacred day, although not fully grasping how sacred until much later.

Because I wasn't fully clear on the meaning and reverence of the Sabbath, how could I expect she would be clear? She believes the Sabbath and frankly all of the Ten Commandments are misunderstood. She said that along with many of her peers, they know them and are aware of them, but aren't necessarily aware of them enough to know whether they misunderstand them. When she was explaining her perspective, it occurred to me that this actually applies to many of us. How do we move from awareness to relevance and reverence for abundance?

What's exciting is that having these conversations with my children is sparking conversations among them and with their friends. They are all precious times for me, and sharing my love of God and His love for them is especially important, so this is a start. I believe they're listening.

When my son Walker has something to say, usually it's simple and to the point. When I asked him if he thought the Ten Commandments were misunderstood, without hesitation, he said, "Not really." I was left hanging, grinning ear-to-ear, and laughing a little because I really couldn't wait for his backup comments. What's the supporting documentation to this response?

"Not really?" I asked him what he meant, and his next answer was equally awesome. He went on to say that they're pretty simple to understand. "Just take them at face value, and don't complicate it. If it says don't steal, then don't steal. There's no wiggle room here, Mama." We do often complicate things that really aren't complicated. So from my three children's points of view, they're misunderstood although simply stated, not complicated, and guardrails for our protection.

Do we have a responsibility to ourselves and to our community to continue this standard of remembering the Sabbath? Other than attending church, how do we practically remember? A start for me is intentionally making the decision not to work on Sundays. When I began to unravel the deeply woven threads connecting me to my business, it was a first step in setting a boundary.

This included not checking business emails (still a challenge), not returning business calls, and not scheduling appointments. This helped kick-start the pattern of awareness, and then awareness led to practice, and that practice then led to my new routine. My heart focused on the Lord and what He wanted me to hear, experience, and enjoy for one day. I continued all my daily devotionals and prayer time the other six days of the week, but Sundays have become the day I look forward to, knowing I get to rest in it all day long with the Lord. Doesn't that sound amazing?

If we find ourselves outside the guardrails, how do we get back in? I suspect there are countless ways to stay inside the guardrails like reading the Word, engaging in Christlike community, and spending time in daily prayer and worship. But getting back in after a season of falling over the rails may be overwhelming. If you start taking inventory of the sins you've committed, don't let that deter you from knowing God wants us inside with Him. I don't believe He's keeping track. Starting small with prayer, a devotional, and heck, even movies are ways God uses to help us hear Him. Although not a prophet and not Moses, Charlton Heston and *The Ten Commandments* movie was a tool the Lord used for me to reacquaint myself with His guardrails each year, down to this day! The message was the truth, God's truth: laws for us, His children, to follow for an abundant life. He loves us, wants us to experience joy, and desires to draw us into close relationship with Him. There are Ten Commandments; start with the first one. Know there is one God who loves you and wants to pour abundance over you.

WHAT ARE YOUR THOUGHTS?

1) Describe when you remember first learning about the Ten Commandments. Have they remained a guardrail for you?

_____

_____

_____

_____

2) Is it difficult for you to honor the Sabbath Day? What barriers keep you from fully engaging in rest? What can you do to remove these barriers?

_____

_____

_____

_____

3) Do you believe the Ten Commandments are misunderstood? Explain how.

_____

_____

_____

_____

4) What helps you stay inside the guardrails? Is there an area that's challenging you?

_____

_____

_____

_____

TWO

MYTHS AND CONSEQUENCES

> Know therefore that the Lord your God is God;
> he is the faithful God, keeping his covenant of
> love to a thousand generations of those who love
> him and keep his commandments.
> —Deuteronomy 7:9

What myths do you believe about God and His Commandments? Is His personality a mystery to you? Is He funny? Witty? Jolly? Or is He huffy and haughty? Is He in heaven watching us fumble around in the world giggling with emotions of endearment? Or is He possibly irritated with us, shaking His head as He watches us make poor choices? I don't believe God is like the latter at all—completely the opposite, as a matter of fact. God unconditionally loves us and is rooting for us always, although I do believe He has a wonderful sense of humor!

I asked my friend Tim, an elder at our church (shout out MCC), what myths he believes people have about God and the Ten Commandments. He believes there are people who truly don't know God and have a vision of Him as this bully in the sky. Really? A bully? I can actually see what he means, though. If you're not in relationship with God, it can appear that God causes or allows all the bad stuff and suffering in our lives. For example, believing He allowed the broken marriage not to heal, the financial hardships to linger and children to suffer a myriad of pains, some may ask where is God? Why didn't He stop the pain and suffering? Doesn't He care? Yes, absolutely; anything to the contrary is a myth.

God doesn't say, "What goes around comes around," or "Watch out for karma." People can fall into the trap of thinking, *I must have done something wrong* or *I've messed up here big-time, so will He even help me? Why should I follow the Ten Commandments if, when I make a mistake—and I will—God can punish me?* Not getting the promotion, not receiving the answer we were hoping for, and so on, must mean that God is up in the sky saying, "Yep, well, I told you so; you've gone and messed up, so that stinks for you!" Is this our God? Is He a bully in the sky waiting for us to mess up? Or worse … does He provoke us, taunt us or put us in intentional situations just to see how we handle them all for his fodder? *No!*

When we hear people say they're God-fearing, is this what they mean? They really are afraid because God is this scary, mean being who wants to celebrate when we fail? And we have failed, we do fail, and we will fail again! Does this mean a life of walking on eggshells because we don't want to bring attention to ourselves in fear that God will notice and pounce at the opportunity to punish us and say, "I told you to follow My commandments, but you ignored Me"? We are sinners, and it's inevitable that we will fall short, so is this what we have to look forward to? A bully in the sky waiting to punish us, taunt us, or tease us? Well, of course not! That's why it's a myth! This may seem silly to some of us who know our wonderful loving Father, but we have to acknowledge the reality of this legitimate misconception.

When visiting with my children about God's unconditional love, I've made a relatable comparison that God's love is like a parent's love. He is our parent, our Father! There are sadly some who've not known true unconditional love from an earthly parent, but they are, however, able to still give it if they are willing. For those of us blessed to have known incredible unconditional love from a parent and been given the gift to be a parent, I've described God's love to my children like this: "Have I ever set you up to fail? Intentionally? Have I ever laughed at your mistakes?"

Well, maybe once, yes, I did laugh when Ellie fell though the display of Christmas boxes in Nordstrom's, but it was *really* funny and we all laughed because it was *really* funny! I shouldn't have laughed, and when I realized Ellie wasn't laughing with us and instead was very embarrassed, I snapped out of it. I chased Ellie into the bathroom, squeezed her tight, and apologized for laughing at her expense. I assured her that I was so very sorry for laughing and assured her I wouldn't ever want to hurt her.

That said, when my children make a mistake, I'm not ready to shake my finger in their face. Have I allowed them to make mistakes? Yes, and God too allows us to make mistakes. Do I try and stop them before I see them going in a direction that may not yield a positive result? Yes. I believe God tries to stop us too by offering the tools we need in His Word and by the Holy Spirit living in us. Parents don't dream up "tests" for our children to see how they perform, and neither does God. That's not indicative of a parent's love on earth or in heaven.

Are there additional myths about the Ten Commandments? Absolutely! There are many, but one that has caused much confusion is that God created the Ten Commandments to condemn us. This is a little like the previous myth but takes it a step farther. My ever-wise stepfather, Fr Jim McLean, said, "The Ten Commandments weren't meant to condemn us. God wrote them to support us and strengthen us and our relationship with God." I believe this is worth repeating;

"The Ten Commandments weren't meant to condemn us. God wrote them to support us and strengthen us and our relationship with God."

If you don't know God as loving, this idea can be confusing. How do we grow in our relationship with God because of the Ten Commandments, which to some seem like a bunch of irrelevant rules? To others they may not seem relevant until as rule breakers they try to use them as ammunition to justify at their whim. It could seem they aren't necessarily taken seriously, unless an earthly consequence is looming. Then they might use them to their advantage or attempt to interpret them to adapt to their situation. So here in lies the culmination of naysayers, know-it-alls, and negotiators. We can doubt the relevance and importance of the Ten Commandments, we can decide which ones matter based on our personal views, or we can be artful in our justifications of the Ten Commandments. Which one are you: naysayer, know-it-all, or negotiator?

Dawson made a similar comparison to the point made by Fr Jim, aka Granddaddy Jim; "They're not meant to condemn us or punish us. They're like our parents' rules, *meant to protect us and to give us a better life. They're guidelines to give us a more fulfilling life, not a restrictive, unexciting life.* Look at them positively, not negatively. God isn't a controlling God. We have free will to follow them or not. They're there to help us because He loves us." So proud he gets it (insert heart), and also, it's true!

Often we don't like the rules and take it upon ourselves to decide which ones apply to us especially if we don't like them. My friend Tina once said, "If you have a challenge with the rules, talk to the person who made the rule." I love this! How many of us would actually strike up a conversation with God and ask Him why we can't spread lies about our neighbor or use His name in vain? Likely not many of us would question His rules if placed in that situation. We may not always like following *His* rules, but are we to question their legitimacy or gravity? As with most parents, the rules are established for a reason, and it's up to us to have faith in their significance for our well-being and that of our children. Translate this to the Ten Commandments and voilà, trusting in them is significant for our well-being too.

The myth that God is like a policeman in the sky with his clipboard ready to pull us over and say, "Hey, stop, you've broken the law. Now I have to give you a consequence"—is this the character of our God? Is He lurking around the corners waiting to give us a citation when we sin? Can you picture this scene: God in His divine regalia, hiding in a regal stance waiting to catch us? News flash: God is everywhere—around the corners, in front of us with us in plain view—and we aren't hidden from Him. He sees it all, and I don't believe He's on patrol waiting to "bust us." I believe because He knows we will sin and we are disobedient, He is, however, there waiting to comfort us when we realize our errors. He loves us regardless of the mistakes we make, just as I love my children, no matter what mistakes they make.

I didn't have rules to make my children miserable, although they may argue otherwise. Their father and I had rules in place to protect them, sometimes from situations that were dangerous:

 - Don't run out into the street—don't talk to strangers.

Or sometimes it was protection from unhealthy choices:

 - No you can't eat donuts and chips for dinner. — No sleepovers on a school night

And sometimes it was to protect them from themselves:

- No running with scissors. — No, you can't go because it isn't safe.

I remember a time when Walker was in eighth or ninth grade. I was with a friend and knew he was with friends too. What I didn't know yet, long story short, was where he and his friends had decided to go, and I intended to find out. I love how GPS sheds light on the most devious plans. I happened to double-check where Walker said he was, and where he actually was jived. They sort of did, but in a well-planned omission, Walker was somewhere he knew wouldn't please me. So, needless to say, I alerted Walker I was on my way to get him. I'm not sure if he was angrier with me for messing up his fun or possibly embarrassing him. No I didn't make a scene, but Walker grudgingly got in the car, and my typically obedient son was clearly in need of expressing his disdain. After a few minutes of blowing off steam, we were home, and less than ten minutes later Walker was in his comfy clothes, nestled under blankets, eating popcorn and watching one of his favorite TV shows. He was safe, comfortable, content and arguably happy(ier). I saved Walker from himself and a potentially uncomfortable peer situation. I knew a better course for him even though it didn't seem that way to him in the moment. He later saw the blessing of my protection. Similarly, God protects us through His commandments.

Every generation has experimented with bucking the system. I can remember way back in my teens, there were a few times I would sneak out. Yes, I had a curious side, and yes, I broke the rules. I didn't break the big ones though, just the milder ones like sneaking out to meet my friends. I can't exactly recall how many times I snuck out, which should tell you something, but what I do remember is that each time I snuck out, the fear of the consequences wasn't enough to stop me. I was more interested in what I would miss out on by staying home. There was "FOMO" in the 1970s and '80s too. Did I ever get in serious trouble away from the safety of my home? No, no accidents or incidents, but I had a few close calls. I can admit that I always felt a little bit bad about breaking the rules. I knew it was wrong.

One night in particular I felt bad because I got caught! There's nothing like being caught to shift your perspective. I can vividly remember how it felt to be disappointing my mom, and if my father had still been living, he would have been disappointed too. When I started explaining the circumstances to my mom, I remember an interesting calm from her. She just listened and let me talk. The more I talked, the more I felt her love. I was so ashamed, yet she didn't say anything to make me feel worse. As a matter of fact, what she said was "Well, I'm glad you told me. Why don't you go on to bed? It's late."

So I went to my room, literally dumbfounded. There was no yelling, no fumes coming from her ears or rage in her eyes. What was happening? I kept thinking, *She's got to be stewing on this*, and the harsh words and punishment were coming. Nothing even close to that happened, and what did happen was by far the worst punishment I could have received. My mom came in my room, tucked me in, gave me a hug, and told me she loved me. Wow! I was so confused, and instead of thinking, *Well cool, I just got off easy,* I asked my mom if I was getting a consequence. To this day, over forty years later, I can still remember what she said. "No! Not unless you feel like you should have one." I was speechless from her mercy.

It was the most effective consequence I could have been issued. I was loved so unconditionally that she, in a moment, forgave me and just loved me. I suffered a consequence anyway. It was the knowledge that I had been selfish, reckless, and all at the expense of disappointing my mom and frankly myself. There are consequences for our sins; there are consequences for breaking the rules and the law, God's Law and the laws of the world. When we don't follow God's commandments, we're breaking the rules, the rules He put in place to protect us and bring us joy. Much like my mom, I believe God is just sitting back calmly listening to us turn ourselves in; true confessions at their best. All the while He still loves us and forgives us, even though we sin. And even when the sin is bigger than sneaking out, He loves us, and when we ask, He forgives us and grants us mercy.

In certain situations when I couldn't fully understand why I wasn't comfortable allowing my children to do this or that, I trusted what the Holy Spirit was telling me. The Holy Spirit convicts us, and listening to our convictions leads to trust. Even when I couldn't explain it, I learned to ask my children to trust me. We see what our children can't see. Our Father sees what we can't see. So often God closes a door or says no to a prayer because His will is far better. A good prayer is for a desire for our will to align with His will and for us to trust Him for His purposes. God is trustworthy! I believe the myth questioning whether we can fully trust God is easily debunked. He never fails us, never leaves us, and is always for us.

I've heard it said that our brains don't fully develop until we're twenty-five. So until then, parents help children navigate murky waters in order to bring them as much joy and ease in their lives as possible. Like our children, we aren't fully developed spiritually in understanding God's character or His Commandments He wrote for us. I believe many of us think we know them just fine, but is this a myth? Do we know them just fine? As there are many myths and misconceptions, do we underestimate the weight of the Ten Commandments? Are we confused by what they mean?

They tend to be interpreted in different ways as routinely

as God is misinterpreted. "You shall not take the name of the Lord your God in vain…" (Exodus 20:7). For most of my life the meaning of this commandment has been simple and literal: I shouldn't say God's name in a blasphemous way. With zero thought or research it was clear to me that this was a pretty simple commandment to keep. If I don't swear the ultimate swear statement using God's name or the name of Jesus, I've achieved success in not breaking this commandment. Right? The self-proclaimed Ten Commandments know-it-all in me believed I was right, and anyone who swore that way was not only foul-mouthed but lewd in character in my mind, breaking one of the easiest commandments to keep.

But what if I'm wrong and there's more to the meaning than I initially understood? Have you ever considered this question? Is there a myth to the meaning of "You shall not take the name of the Lord in vain"? Do you believe you've taken the name of the Lord our God in vain or avoided breaking this particular commandment? If you can sincerely say that you've never said, "Oh My God," "Oh My Gosh," "OMG," "Jeez," and even the old standby "Golly Gee," I'm impressed! I've said them all—a lot, so evidently I've broken this commandment a lot!

The word *gosh* was introduced into the English language in the mid-1700s, followed by *golly* and *gee* in the 1800s. These words were not just cheeky expressions of attitude, but actually derivatives of the words God and Jesus. Who knew? When we say or text "OMG," we're technically saying, "Oh my God," or in my case saying, "Jeez" and "Oh my gosh." I've not thought I was dishonoring God. But apparently I might have been all along, and so has my Ellie! (Sorry for calling you out, honey.) She recently shared a sweet story of being at our family friend's house in Nashville hanging out with their three young daughters. One of the little girls was telling her a story, and Ellie slipped out an

"Oh my gosh!" In an instant Ellie was called out by a seven-year-old that she wasn't supposed to say that and might get in trouble. Ellie retorted back that she hadn't said, "Oh My God," but "Oh My Gosh." Well that wasn't allowed either, Margaret hastened to report. Ellie couldn't wait to tell me, mostly because she knew I was literally writing about the Ten Commandments, and the timing was awesome, but also this was simply hilarious. "Out of the mouth of babes" lives on!

We so often commonly express our attitudes and emotions with OMG and its many iterations that it's easy to see how it's become no big deal to say it or hear it said. In the marketplace, if you search for OMG, you'll find endless options donning the abbreviated expression. OMG coffee mugs, OMG candles, OMG T-shirts—it goes on and on. In full transparency I saw several pieces that I thought were so cute and clever I could have ordered them for my house.

It's now beyond a phenomenon to use such speech and if anything becoming the norm. "OMG, did you see that outfit?" "Oh God, that was a scary movie!" "Oh my gosh, I'm still full from that incredible dinner last night," "Oh Lordy." I've said 'em all, while completely unaware I was blaspheming God. I've probably been unaware because I wasn't saying them with the intention of being contemptuous of God. Believing myself off the hook, maybe I've diluted the reverence of these expressions by overusing them and using them too casually to notice anymore. Can you relate, or is it just me?

Conversely, if I were to say, "Oh my God, why has this happened to me?" prayerfully, is that different? I personally believe it is very different and a direct intentional plea to the Lord for answers. When we're speaking with the Lord and praying to Him, saying His name with high honor, there's a definite regard to His holiness and a difference of tone. If the same statement is said blaming God or using His name in anger or frustration with Him specifically, then maybe that's the sin. It's our hearts, our tone, and the intention behind our words possibly that break this commandment.

I question how our use of these few words has morphed into seemingly irreverent and sacrilegious language. I also question what we do about it. God is the Almighty, our Lord and Holy One. He deemed important as a Commandment to regard His name for a reason; otherwise, why have it as a commandment? For us to toss His name around with little or no thought is sloppy. Doesn't God deserve our utmost honor and reverence? His name is holy, beautiful and perfect, the name above *all* names, so why has it become such a cavalier habit to disregard His name in how we use it?

More so, what if calling ourselves Christians could be considered taking the name of the Lord in vain? Saying we are Christians but not living like Christ, are we sinning, taking the name of the Lord in vain? I'm certainly not attempting to redefine what it means to be a Christian. I'm also not certain if it's blasphemous to say, "I am a Christian," if my heart does not reflect His ways. I do, however, buy into the notion that to call ourselves Christian and then, "behind the comma," to say something contrary to being Christlike is worth raising an eyebrow. Statements like "I'm a Christian, but if that happened to me I would never forgive them," or "I'm a Christian, but I don't need to go to church," or "I'm a Christian, but I'm private about my faith and don't need to share it with others"—does this sound like Christ? Paul tried to encourage the people of Corinth to be like him, imitating Christ; we should also be imitators of Christ, "Be imitators of me, as I am of Christ" (1 Corinthians 11:1).

Even when I believed I was doing all right keeping this commandment, apparently I wasn't. I've sinned and sinned and sinned using the Lord's name in vain, although I've not intended to. This commandment is often shortened when spoken, but the full commandment written in Exodus says, "You shall not take the name of the Lord your God in vain, for the Lord will not hold him guiltless who takes his name in vain."

There are those who have rejected God and will not know grace and mercy according to His Commandment. This is a grave reality and sobering to digest! It saddens me for these souls, and it scared me for a moment as I dug deep into realizing my own sin. I had let down our Father, hurt Him, and sinned against Him, and all with little knowledge of my error. It hurt me that I had hurt Him, and then I feared for my salvation as the Commandment says the Lord will not hold him guiltless. Will He forgive me? In the most humble of moments, I realized, yes, I would be forgiven. I almost couldn't bear my emotions of gratitude for our Savior's grace.

One of the many blessings in being a Christian is there's no shame. God knows our hearts. When we confess our sins and ask for forgiveness, He forgives us. First John 1:9 says, "If we confess our sins, he is faithful and just to forgive us our sins and to cleanse us from all unrighteousness." Amen, and thank You, Father!

If we acknowledge we don't want to use the name of the Lord in vain, how do we break the habit? What do we say instead? What first steps should we take to develop awareness and change the word choices that roll off our tongues without thinking? Praying about it is step one. Asking God to forgive us for using His name in vain and asking the Holy Spirit to convict our hearts to uphold this commandment is a priority. Continue praying for His help, and I am certain change will happen.

Write down several phrases and words to use as substitutes like "My stars," "Oh my," or one my mom often says, "Well, hot dog!" There are endless options, so have fun creating alternatives.

And the next time you let out an "OMG" or a "Jeez" or say "I'm a Christian," don't be too hard on yourself. We all fall short of perfection! I caught myself saying, "Jeez" and "Oh my gosh" at least twice just yesterday, so it's not an easy habit to break, but it got me thinking of about my intentions when I said it. My advice is to pause and consider why you used God's name, what could you have said instead, and how it made you feel to say it. Then consider asking God to forgive you for using His name in vain if in fact you did. I know I will do all of the above again and again and again, as His perfect name is no myth!

Pastor Nick told me another common myth often believed is that if we try to obey the Ten Commandments, we are saved. "The Ten Commandments reveal our need to be saved, but if you're a 'good person' and try to be a follower, without Jesus, you're not saved." Through the blood of Jesus is the only way to salvation.

Romans 10:9–10 says, "because, if you confess with your mouth that Jesus is Lord and believe in your heart that God raised him from the dead, you will be saved. For with the heart one believes and is justified, and with the mouth one confesses and is saved." It's important for us to understand it's by our hearts and our mouths that we are saved. Nick shares that the church struggles to help us understand that obedience to the Ten Commandments doesn't save us. You may be wondering, what's the point of obeying them if they don't affect our salvation? If we have a launch pad or a home base for truth, then we know there's a place to go for wisdom, answers, and direction. We also know that by abiding by His commandments, we are in closer relationship with the Lord, which translates to a multitude of blessings.

If we start by honoring God's commandments, then we are headed in the right direction. That said, it's when we "follow" the Ten Commandments as works and a plan to gain eternal life that we miss the mark. This is the myth. I can't tell you how many times I've heard it said, "I'm a good person, I believe in God, and basically I try to do the right thing and do good deeds for others, so that should get me into heaven." The challenge with this thinking is you have to be saved for your eternal salvation, number one! And the irony is while some people are running around being "good," it doesn't give them a get-into-heaven pass. But those who have never heard the gospel but have just experienced discipleship and received Jesus have a definite path to salvation. They have truly learned to know God's loving mercy, decided to ask God for forgiveness, accepted His Son as their Savior, and have eternal life.

It's important to differentiate between goodness and obedience. Being obedient to God's Word will bring abundance and blessings far more rewarding than being good will ever deliver.

God knew we would fall short, and that's why He sacrificed His Son for our sins. That said, He still asks us to follow His laws. Realizing we can't successfully ignore or hide from God is a good start to trusting and having a closer relationship with Him. When we disobey our parents and hide our shame, mistakes, and bad choices from them, they somehow find out. God, however, finds out all the time because we can't hide anything from Him. This is what amazes me when I sit back and think about it. We tend to make choices, some more significant than others, that aren't always good for us, and we aren't fooling God! He loves us no matter what and will comfort us, provide for us, and forgive us if we ask Him.

Walker and I were talking about myths of the Ten Commandments, and his thoughts were direct and made me think. He said, "There's no myth. They mean what they mean. People sometimes start thinking of them differently, and that's when it can get complicated and make religion look hypocritical." What? Religion has hypocrites? He goes on to say, "It can look hypocritical because how we live doesn't always match what we call ourselves." Another proud mama moment! And this ties us back into the myth of calling ourselves Christians as a sin. How we look and act and what we say are tied to our hearts, motivations, and intentions. If we start interpreting the Ten Commandments to mean what we need them to mean to fit our circumstances, then the myth has taken over that the Ten Commandments are flexible. I wonder if God sees it that way. After all, He wrote them in stone, and when He wrote them, I imagine He was very clear about their meaning. There's no myth or misconception about that!

WHAT ARE YOUR THOUGHTS?

1) Does the relationship you have with your parents affect the relationship you have with God?

_____

_____

_____

_____

2) If there was a myth you could dispel about the Ten Commandments, what would it be?

_____

_____

_____

_____

3) Have you had a misconception about using the name of the Lord in vain? How does it make you feel?

_____

_____

_____

_____

4) How will you go forward regarding God's Fourth Commandment about taking the name of the Lord in vain?

_____

_____

_____

_____

THREE

SELF-RIGHTEOUS CHECKLIST

> There is only one Lawgiver and Judge, the one
> who is able to save and destroy. But you who are
> you to judge your neighbor?
>
> —James 4:12

There was a time in history when the subject of God was the center of many conversations. The Bible teaches us when knowing right versus wrong or understanding laws and traditions was seemingly to proclaim God's truth. There were wars and upheavals over religious convictions, who and what to worship, and interpretations over beliefs of His laws.

This is still happening today in many countries including in America. Controversies about God in schools, God in our government, and Right to Life in all its many facets are all fluid real-time discussions in our nation. No matter your personal side of the conversation, it's often a morphing display of the best in us and the worst in us, primarily because whatever *we* believe in is right! All the while we battle the knee-jerk judgment of all who oppose our point of view. On the one hand, we have our personal convictions, yet on the other hand how do we align our convictions with expanding His kingdom if we don't all agree to at least talk about it?

It's ironic to realize that debates and controversies of this and greater magnitude were happening in the first century about Jesus, and here we are thousands of years later still sorting through the meaning of God and His relevance in our lives. Those of us, who believe Jesus is our Savior and call ourselves Christians, express our beliefs in a variety of ways. Some of us wear our faith boldly from a cross necklace to a tattoo of a cross or scripture on our bodies, or we display a cross or scripture in our homes and on T-shirts. Expressions like these may even be a first step for a new believer to manifest his or her love of the Lord tangibly, which is awesome!

Where does this expression stop and start, however? Are we only comfortable wearing our beliefs versus talking about God with our colleagues, friends, and family? With the genesis of social media, it may be easy to share our faith virtually, but perhaps for some it's awkward to post about God. Sharing who we really are and what matters to us can be thwarted by unknown opinions from not only the social media police, but also from the people closest to us. Do we shy away from revealing our faith in certain company or certain situations like at a dinner party? If so, why? Maybe we could be met with naysayers or the feeling of not being prepared to engage in a battle of the wits in defense of our convictions. No matter the reason, it seems as if talking about God to our peers has become taboo: the untouchable subject: the potentially offensive or uncomfortable conversation to have and in essence living with a secret passion. Has talking about God gotten "the boot" and being religious become a passé topic?

I think not! I sense a noticeable shift into revival—praise the Lord! By the time I publish this book, my prayer is that millions of new believers and followers of Christ will have been born, and God will be rightly worshipped! I also pray that we will become comfortable again to make the talking about our faith as "normal" as discussing our diets, exercise routines, financial goals or personal family matters. A recent Barna Poll study from May 2021 stated that over 51 percent of 1,000 polled believe in a biblical worldview, and 78 percent believe God cares a lot about them and what they think. Conversely, the same poll revealed that 76 percent believe being "good" gets them into heaven, and 95 percent don't believe obedience to God produces success (which to me is relative to your definition of success).

I look at these poll results as an opportunity for us to talk about God more openly and piggyback on the conversations that I'm personally witnessing all around me. The number of Christians in America may have been declining in recent years according to one poll, but I can't help notice the increase in God's "popularity" on my social media feed. This has to mean something! Whether it's current events stirring the souls of His children or all part of God's plan remains to be understood. For my part, I'm an optimistic observer continuing to pray for the expansion of disciples and do my part for His glory.

There've been numerous occasions where I've tiptoed around the subject of God with people I care about—not because I was embarrassed at how I felt, but because I was concerned with a certain awkwardness to "not go there," as it's seemingly too personal, too private for others. In my head I'm thinking, *More private than hearing about their sex life or marriage? More private than discussing friends' most personal pain with others in judgment?* These thoughts began awakening in my soul. It started to feel uncomfortable being in conversations that had nothing to do with me. Engaging in silent agreement became uncomfortable too. I still heard the conversations, so I felt like a participant even though I didn't ask to be. I've witnessed, participated in, and experienced all sides of this particular judgment.

Recently with a group of friends, I had an epiphany. Even in the closest and most comfortable dynamics, there's judgment and a self-righteous impression for what is morally allowed and what isn't. From social justice to civil liberties, there's a code that some would have us or even command us to follow for their comfort, yet we are condemned if we're not in agreement. We can be persecuted for following God's laws and especially condemned for breaking them *if* they don't fit a narrative in sync with opposing beliefs, but what about my beliefs? When do I stay silent, and when do I speak up?

For the sake of not ruffling feathers, I sometimes still stay silent despite my personal convictions, and in this situation, I still did. Why? The words of Matthew 7:1–2, "Do not judge, or you too will be judged. For in the same way you judge others, you will be judged, and with the measure you use, it will be measured to you," began to pierce my spirit. If I am listening, agreeing, or even remaining, silent, it's as if I was in agreement and participating in the judgment of others' sins. Has this become the norm, and are we to accept that? My instinct, as I matured spiritually, was not to be a part of unhealthy and unloving conversations. If you're wondering what this has to do with the Ten Commandments, it's this; how we see our neighbors' sins and how we view our sins remind me of a self-righteous sin checklist. Placing an *X* next to our neighbor's name who we believe has broken a commandment, and placing a check mark next to our own name under commandments we've kept, equals judgment. "You shall not take vengeance or bear a grudge against the sons of your own people, but you shall love your neighbor as yourself: I am the Lord" (Leviticus 19:18).

Being judged, knowingly or not, and judging others, raises the question, have you ever cheated, lied, stolen, gossiped, sworn, hated, or felt envy? If you're like me, you're going down the checklist trying to justify if you've judged and what commandments you have or haven't broken. If we can stand a little taller with relief for not committing the really bad ones, like murder and stealing, it's possibly easier to justify our scale on less serious sins like adultery, although it may be deemed worse than taking the name of the Lord in vain by many standards. Does the order of the Ten Commandments dictate which ones are indeed worse than others, or does the order mean anything at all?

This and many other questions have me wondering. If I reference the Bible, including multiple translations, one thing is consistent. "I am the Lord your God" is the first commandment. The remaining nine are positioned roughly the same, but I find it interesting is that in all translations I've seen, the order has "You shall not murder," "You shall not steal," and "You shall not commit adultery" after "You shall not take the name of the Lord in vain," "Remember the Sabbath day, to keep it holy," and "Honor your father and your mother." Why do we as a society issue a higher consequence and moral judgment on those who've committed murder, adultery, and stealing?

Since there's an order to how God spoke the Ten Commandments, I propose giving at the very least double check marks to any person who doesn't take the name of the Lord in vain, remembers the Sabbath, or honors their father and mother to adjust the checklist curve we tend to follow. This may sound silly, but I am a fan of good getting more points than bad if making our own rules in our checklist game. If we are tempted to assign our own grades and grade our neighbor, it's logical! Obviously I'm not being serious, but my negotiator mind could justify this all day long.

ESV BIBLE-Protestant	CATHOLIC	JEWISH
1- I am the Lord your God. You will have no other gods before me	I am the Lord your God. You shall not have any strange gods before me	I am the Lord thy God
2-You shall not make for yourself a carved image	You shall not take the Lord your God in vain	You shall have no other gods before me
3-You shall not take the name of the Lord your God in vain	Remember to keep holy the Lord's day	Thou shall not take the name of the Lord in vain.
4-Remember the Sabbath day, to keep it holy.	Honor your father and your mother	Remember the Sabbath day to keep it holy
5-Honor your father and your mother.	You shall not kill	Honor thy father and thy mother.
6-You shall not murder	You shall not commit adultery	Thou shall not murder
7-You shall not commit adultery	You shall not steal	Thou shall not commit adultery
8-You shall not steal	You shall not bear false witness against your neighbor	Thou shall not steal
9-You shall not bear false witness against your neighbor.	You shall not covet your neighbor's wife	Thou shall not bear false witness against thy neighbor.
10-You shall not covet.	You shall not covet your neighbor's goods.	Thou shall not covet anything that belongs to thy neighbor.

*There are many more interpretations of the Ten Commandments order. Even within religions they can be worded differently. This chart is exhibits one example.

If we take a look at the chart there are modest variations and places where the commandments are listed in different orders. What isn't a variation is acknowledging our one true God is nonnegotiable: always first! I believe God was intentional in how He told the Commandments to Moses, so they're in this order for a reason. It mattered to God, so it should matter to us. We may not know the reason for His order as the order doesn't necessarily correlate with some being worse than others. What we may want to reexamine is why our default is to pin particular judgment on certain sins.

As a society we have decided on what sins matter most and their respective relevance. We've established legal consequences for certain laws and definite moral judgments on the backs of people in reflection of our hearts or, worse, foolishness. We've decided that we can commit certain sins and negotiate the severity for ourselves. As I mentioned earlier, we negotiate our consequences at times, and as classified sin know-it-alls and negotiators, we often decide how to grade ourselves when going through the sin checklist. Example: Remembering the Sabbath could come across not nearly as bad as murder. I'm a good person who tries to remember the Sabbath and haven't murdered, so check that sin in the "No" column with a "?" next to remembering the Sabbath. What other boxes can I check? What boxes can you and have you checked?

If I'm being honest, murder is one of the Ten Commandments that I've proudly never committed. I've checked the box: nope, never murdered. Good girl, pat myself on the back. Or can I? It is written in scripture that having anger in our heart, harboring wicked thoughts, or wishing ill will toward our brother, although a matter of our hearts, is still murder. "You have heard that it was said to those of old 'You shall not murder; and whoever murders will be liable to judgment.' But I say to you that everyone who is angry with his brother will be liable to judgment... " (Matthew 5:21–22). "But what comes out of the mouth proceeds from the heart, and this defiles a person. For out of the heart come evil thoughts, murder, adultery, sexual immorality, theft, false witness, slander" (Matthew 15:18–19).

If this is true, and having hate in our hearts or wishing ill will with intent towards our brother, literal or otherwise, means we are murderers, then I have to admit I'm guilty of unfair judgment and not innocent of this sin. It's also convenient for us to reference these and other scriptures when we need a good dose of justification. "Whoever takes a human life shall surely be put to death" (Leviticus 24:17). This too is extremely controversial. Depending on the biblical translation, this commandment is either "Thou shalt not kill" or "You shall not murder." There's a difference, I believe. According to some points of view, killing applies to everything from people to plants and animals. I'm not certain what God meant when issuing this commandment, because there are multiple places in scripture where He goes into detail on how to sacrifice an animal and enter into battle with the intent of killing the enemy. It can get murky, I suppose, if we consider war, defending our property, defending ourselves, and hunting for our families' survival, all killing for good reasons.

In the Old Testament death by killing is the consequence for many broken laws. It's incredibly controversial but worthwhile to work out where to stand on these questions, but more importantly where you believe God stands. Since our Savior, Jesus, died for us, we have a path to be forgiven as a murderer, both literally and of the heart. I believe it always comes back to our heart and our intent. For the one who's murdered, committed a crime, and suffered consequences past or present, there's mercy available. Hearts can change if open to receiving God's free gift of grace.

One of the most worthy outreach ministries available in many churches and communities is the prison ministry. I've heard countless stories of the gospel being preached in fellowship with inmates there for a variety of crimes. Accepting Christ, and experiencing love and mercy for the first time, frees us from shame and forgives all sins including murder. Our goal as Christians is to expand God's kingdom, so as fellow sinners we ought not write off the murderer as irredeemable or worse than us by sin standards, although I'm challenged to get there with the most wicked of criminals. We can't get stuck in the tunnel of categorizing sins. We must remember that our God is the same God who loves all His children and wrote *all* of the commandments for all us to follow.

One of the many lessons I've embraced throughout this journey is the grace God extends to all of us, no matter what our sin. In that vein, if God isn't fully classifying or quantifying our sins, why do we keep hypothetical checklists of our own actions and those of others? In establishing an order of severity, we might not be getting it right, and the checklists we've been operating from could be outdated. It's worth revisiting at the very least to be sure we add humility, mercy, and grace to our checklists to keep us, well—in check.

I was curious what my wise mentor, Joye, thought about there being an order to the Ten Commandments and if some were worse than others. Her perspective resonated with me; "Yes," she believes there is an order. Like the many translations of the Bible, Joye agrees that the first commandment is God is Lord, and we are to love Him first above all others. The second, according to Matthew 22:39, is to love our neighbors. And then she added that all the commandments support the first two.

She highlighted those I call the sin know-it-alls next by saying she believed people focus on the sins they don't believe they commit as those that are the worst. In other words, we don't like to look at our sins but we don't mind pointing out those of others. And of course those are much worse than any we would commit: all of course tongue in cheek, but such a "wow" perspective to consider.

To this end, a common sin we label as a society is the adulterous sinner. These are some of the worst sinners of all, right up there with murderers, according to how they're treated. We condemn, slander, gossip, and pretty much drag adulterers through the proverbial mud. It's true adultery is a sin, and yes, it's true that it's not good. But is it worse than not remembering the Sabbath day, using the name of the Lord in vain, or not honoring our father and mother? "Let anyone among you who is without sin be the first to throw a stone at her" (John 8:7). Are we the ones throwing the stones or perhaps being hit by them?

If you've committed adultery, it's possible you've experienced enormous shame and persecution. I've witnessed this persecution toward adultery, both intentional and unintentional. I say unintentional because I believe there are people who don't want to be a part of the persecution but may not have the courage to speak up in an awkward situation or stand up for the one under attack. When I learn about people's private pain in a public way, I can't help but think about *The Scarlet Letter*. This book is the acclaimed novel written in the mid-1800s by Nathaniel Hawthorne. The story is about a woman who bears a child as a result of an affair. She is persecuted for committing adultery and required to wear a scarlet *A* so all will know her sin. Can you imagine if we required that today? The shame many women wear is pretty bright and significant as it is, even though not literally displayed.

It would be interesting if all sinners had to wear a giant letter representing their sins. The blasphemer calling out the "cheater" while uttering the name of the Lord in vain and bearing false witness against their neighbor—what letter would they publicly have to don?—a *G* for gossiping about the neighbor or a *V* for using the name of the Lord in vain? Or would they need to wear an *A* too, because in their heart they've actually committed adultery?

I always thought that this was a pretty clear and straightforward sin to understand. If you're married, you may not have a voluntary emotional or sexual relationship outside of your marriage. Clear, right? Well, some would say yes, but herein lies the murky part. According to Matthew 5:27–28, "You have heard that it was said, 'You shall not commit adultery.' But I say to you that everyone who looks at a woman with lustful intent has already committed adultery with her in his heart." In this case, porn and lust are considered adultery. Men are called to cherish the wife of their youth. If loving a spouse less and admiring someone else's spouse more than yours is in fact adultery, some stone throwers are actually adulterers too.

Our bodies are God's temples, and of all the commandments, committing adultery is the only one that violates His temple, where the Holy Spirit lives. "Do you not know that your bodies are temples of the Holy Spirit, who is in you, whom you have received from God? You are not your own; you were bought at a price. Therefore honor God with your bodies" (1 Corinthians 6:19–20). It's sobering for me to read this scripture and take in its full meaning. And of course, I've now got even more questions. For one, how do we look at this commandment, our neighbors, and ourselves differently, realizing we've potentially had it all wrong?

A dear friend of mine recently shared that she was angry with a Christian artist for over twenty years because of the artist's divorce. Loving her music—and that of her new husband of over twenty years now—she was still let down by what she judged as the possible reasons behind it all. I've held people to higher standards myself, but all of us are human, celebrities too, and what I love about this particular story my friend shared is that while it let her down (she's now forgiven her), there were others who found redemptive hope through the artist's testimony.

The ruthless scrutiny is dished out oftentimes without knowing circumstances, but this doesn't justify the actions. It's still sin, it still hurts people, and it's wrong. And there is no question that God doesn't want man and wife to break their bond as one in any way. As a matter fact, He is very clear about this in Luke 16:18: "Everyone who divorces his wife and marries another commits adultery, and he who marries a woman divorced from her husband commits adultery." One of my dear friends wondered whether even if the divorce wasn't her fault and she didn't want the divorce, or even if she's "innocent" in the divorce and marries again, is that in fact committing adultery? Is there a loophole here? There's so much shame and social condemnation for having your sin exposed and on display. I was guilty myself of unfairly judging others, until a new perspective was born from knowing this pain much closer to home.

It's curious that we decide how bad a sinner a particular person can be according to the circumstances that led to the sin. In some cases I've heard remarks like "Well, I can't say I'm surprised" or "I don't blame them at all considering X-Y-Z." Joye believes we distinguish consequences in a secular sense and assign a morality to them according to our judgment—although we aren't supposed to be the judge. "Judge not, and you will not be judged; condemn not, and you will not be condemned; forgive, and you will be forgiven …. Why do you see the speck in your brother's eye, but do not notice the log that is in your own eye?" (Luke 6:37, 41). Are we too hard on adulterers, or do they truly have it coming?

The amazing good news is that there is grace! If you love and acknowledge Jesus as your Savior, yes, there is grace, forgiveness, and mercy. As with all sin, asking for forgiveness invites God's mercy and healing, not only within yourself but also with those who have hurt because of this circumstance. I believe it's important that we understand that while the consequences can be painful, there can also be tremendous growth and grace in our circumstances. I've personally had to go through and endure my experiences to fully understand what the Ten Commandments meant. I also believe that through suffering, God has used my brokenness for my gain to His glory. We have the opportunity to grow closer to God, and it's then that He teaches us to open our hearts and our eyes to knowing more about Him, His love, and the love He asks us to have toward others. Witnessing to others after our triumphs will undoubtedly help people find hope and offer us certain healing as we are discipling.

If we forgive ourselves for shame we may feel, forgive others for pain they have caused, and ask forgiveness for those we have hurt, there will be peace. "Be merciful, just as your Father is merciful" (Luke 6:36). And for those of us guilty of persecuting, it's not too late to show mercy, "because judgment without mercy will be shown to anyone who has not been merciful. Mercy triumphs over judgment" (James 2:13). It's important to remember that adultery is one of the Ten Commandments, and God didn't appear to place it as one of the worst; neither should we.

I love what my friend Tim says about the Ten Commandments having an order. He imagines the cross, representing God's relationship with us in the first four commandments, abiding in Him from east to west. All the remaining commandments flow from there as obedience to God and reflect our relationships with our neighbor.

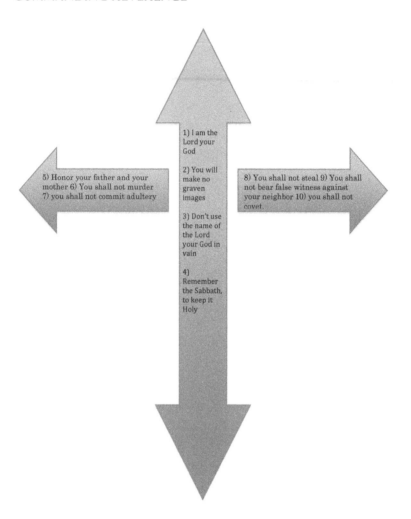

1) I am the Lord your God

2) You will make no graven images

3) Don't use the name of the Lord your God in vain

4) Remember the Sabbath, to keep it Holy

5) Honor your father and your mother 6) You shall not murder 7) you shall not commit adultery

8) You shall not steal 9) You shall not bear false witness against your neighbor 10) you shall not covet.

Our obedience is only possible if we're loving God first. If we love others first and try to be good and do good and rely on others first, the result will be disappointment and broken hearts, but God will never break our heart. Being cautious not to focus on our goodness is paramount in His opinion, because otherwise we run the risk of ironically acting badly like a Pharisee in judgment. Loving others is easier if we love God first. This is such a powerful vision and a wonderful way to illustrate the Ten Commandments.

Although there may not necessarily be an order of severity according to how God sees sin, the commandments do result in different consequences in the world; some of those are in fact worse than others. Whether by our laws or societal consequences, there's a price to pay. Concerning ourselves with others first in whatever form will move us farther away from God and closer to our inner modern-day Pharisee. Choosing to follow God first will move us closer to Him with all our hearts, souls, minds, and strength.

When we are walking with our self-righteous checklist, letting ourselves off the hook and looking for loopholes, it might be time to check our hearts. Truly, the more we grow in our relationship with God, the more our hearts grow toward others. The ease with which we may have once judged, persecuted, and blindly committed sins we negotiated ourselves out of, doesn't feel so good anymore. Again, I believe it is a matter of our hearts. Perhaps there will still be times when righteous anger is in order. We just need to understand the difference between accountability for sin and condemnation. If there's hate in our heart, it's sin. God says the vengeance is His, and He delivers justice, but He also shows us grace, not hellfire and damnation. So why do we sometimes fall into the trap of issuing judgments on others while negotiating our self-righteous checklist of "goodness"?

Do you think it would make a difference if the consequences of breaking God's commands were the same today as they were when God wrote them? I mentioned earlier that the punishment for cursing your father and mother was death. The consequence for adultery and murder was death, unless the murder was unintentional as in self-defense. Almost all of the consequences seem harsh to me today when I read them. Being put to death was not the penalty for many sins, but being shamed and put out from the tribe or camp for many reasons, and experiencing

God's wrath, His disappointment and vengeance, was seemingly common. The Israelites were just a few days away from God's Promised Land of milk and honey, but they continued to do things their way, making their own idols and rules—basically, like many of us today; they decided to evaluate what was worth risking for their purposes rather than trusting God's provisions. As I read the Old Testament and attempt to better understand God's commandments, I am more humbled and grateful than ever for my Savior, Jesus Christ. Without Him, all consequences are death.

Rapid-fire questions are now coming to mind. If today we faced a punishment of death or being outcast from our cities and communities, would we take a harder look at our checklist? Would we pause before we knowingly chose to sin and judge? Do we take forgiveness for granted? In other words, do we justify our sins because we know God will automatically forgive us?

Have we committed more sins than we realize? If we have, perhaps it's time to put down our self-righteous checklists. Instead of looking for loopholes to justify our sins and judging others for theirs, let's not forget that God considers them all sin, and they all made the top ten. While weaning ourselves from negotiating our checklists, God's Word is the perfect resource to follow: "You, then, who teach others, do you not teach yourself? You who preach against stealing, do you steal? You who say that people should not commit adultery, do you commit adultery? You who abhor idols, do you rob temples? You who boast in the law, do you dishonor God by breaking the law?" (Romans 2:21–23).

I love how Ellie answered me when I asked her if she believed there was an order to the Ten Commandments and if some are worse than others. She said that the first and second are the most important, to love God and love thy neighbor, but they are all sin. God sees them all the same. Then she referenced her precious Arkansas Camp Ozark days and the F.I.T. award (First is Third, which she won at least three times; yes, I'm modestly proud). This award is presented to the person from each cabin who most exhibited loving God first, others second, and themselves third. It's such an easy thing to do really; if we focused on these principles, it would be interesting if we continued living with our sin checklist. If we changed our mindset and started loving God first, above all things including ourselves, how would that change the narrative and ignite new conversations toward Christ?

My prayer is, as we're becoming more comfortable and confident in our relationship with God, we will grow more confident to speak the truth about our love and relationship with God with family, friends, and neighbors. We can not only wear our faith on our sleeve, but we can post it, claim it, express it, and watch how our authenticity moves the needle in God's kingdom. I believe He deserves it! "And these words that I command you today shall be on your heart. You shall teach them diligently to your children, and shall talk of them when you sit in your house, and when you walk by the way, and when you lie down, and when you rise" (Deuteronomy 6:6–7).

WHAT ARE YOUR THOUGHTS?

1) Do you tend to negotiate whether you've broken certain Commandments? Which ones have you considered the most important to keep and never break?

_____

_____

_____

_____

2) Which of the Ten Commandments would you strive to follow more if the consequences were like those in the Old Testament?

_____

_____

_____

_____

3) Have you judged anyone too harshly for his or her sins? If so, ask them for forgiveness as you focus on the log in your own eye.

_____

_____

4) Are you comfortable, and do you believe it matters wearing your beliefs about God on your sleeve figuratively and literally?

FOUR

RELIGIOUS BUFFET

"If you love me, you will keep my commandments."
—John 14:15

Do we treat God and our relationship with Him like a religious buffet? When we're in need of a spoonful, dish up? Dawson used this analogy while explaining his point that when certain circumstances suit or justify our needs, a buffet-style religion applies. In other words, we handpick our activeness within our faith walk as adequate or not, according to—well, us.

Justify is an interesting word with multiple meanings. It can mean to prove or show to be just, right, or reasonable. Just means being what is merited or deserved, righteous. For many of us, we decide if we're being reasonable or whether our neighbors and we deserve this assignment of righteousness. I don't believe this is up to us, however. God justifies us with forgiveness, whether we deserve it or not. We have a tendency to attempt justification ourselves and to be our own monitors of righteousness. Some people believe this style religion is sufficient, but to others it may not be a preferred style at all.

There was a time when I was less open about my relationship with God. I went to church most Sundays, made sure my children participated in all the "important" church youth programs, and I was a good person according to my standards of a good person. I genuinely believed this was enough to be a Christian and be all right with God. I was doing what I sincerely felt was the right thing as a believer. I knew there was more depth to a relationship with God, but I had an excuse why that wasn't necessary for me, a justification. I was selecting my style of Christianity and what I believed was a healthy choice for me at the time. I justified my lack of growth based on my acts of "goodness." I was a regular customer at the religious buffet for all the right reasons. But in reality, was it the best deal after all?

I was in such a place in my relationship with God that I occasionally kept it hidden. It's difficult to admit that now, but in that time of my life, I was more concerned with what someone of the world might think of me instead of what God thought of me. I felt a stirring of conflict in my soul and began to notice and have awareness of what following God looked like, and it wasn't me. I still wrestled with justification for some of my decisions, but like many people, I would let myself off the hook for certain sins and not consider those as big a deal as others. So the question then is why not? If we select certain sins to uphold, why not uphold them all? Is it because some of us approach our faith as a religious buffet? "I'll have some coveting please, with a spoonful of lying about my neighbor. Then pepper on worshipping a few false idols like money, and then I'll top off my plate with a heap of calling myself a Christian." Does this sound nutritious to pile on our proverbial plates?

A new and popular restaurant came to town when I was in high school, and they offered the most amazing pizza buffet. I would go often with my childhood besties Katherine and Haven, but in hindsight I'm not sure if the pizza is the reason it was so cool. It could have been the pizza with all the options, the amazing salad bar, the affordable buffet prices, the cute guys that seemed to hang out there (emphasis on cute guys) or all of the above! With the genesis of the buffet and its growing popularity, we became enamored with the convenience and customizations it offered.

This isn't unique to pizza buffets at all. We've subscribed to this lifestyle in many areas of our lives, and I've been the beneficiary of these perks myself and loved it! So what's wrong with convenience and customization and in particular a buffet? Nothing! They're awesome and a great value, as long as we don't overindulge.

When it comes to a religious buffet, however, cherry-picking what we want and when, may not be the best choice. Walking up to the hypothetical buffet line of Commandments and deciding when it's all right to pass up the good, healthy selections and dive into the more enticing choices tends to look like hypocrisy. At a buffet I pass up beets most of the time and the marshmallow salad, but beets are good for us (I'm not sure about the marshmallow salad). I may not want beets, but they have a purpose, and if I add them to my plate, I'll likely be healthier. The Ten Commandments are also good for us, and following them will yield us healthier lives spiritually, emotionally, and physically.

With that in mind, I suspect we often pass up the ones that don't satisfy our desires and serve our agendas, like remembering the Sabbath. In turn, we may opt to consume too much of the ones that are bad for us without counting the sinful calories found in ones such as bearing false witness against our neighbor. Is it possible we don't consider how damaging this is for our soul-filled diet? "You shall not bear false witness against your neighbor" (Exodus 20:16). Not a week goes by that I'm not participating in or witnessing a conversation that doesn't have to do with me. I undoubtedly insert my opinion or two cents regarding the conversation, so does this mean I bear false witness against my neighbor? And who is our neighbor? I'm fairly certain this doesn't only apply to our literal neighbor. If we bear false witness against our neighbor, how can we be loving toward our neighbor at the same time? Does this mean we're actually breaking two commandments at once? If so, this isn't a competition I'm eager to win.

I've always believed this commandment simply meant telling lies about others, but there's much more! To bear false witness also means to gossip, to share information that isn't ours to share, to cause difficulty for someone, and to teach what isn't true. Proverbs 6:16–19, says,

> *There are six things the Lord hates,*
> *seven that are an abomination to Him:*
> *Haughty eyes, a lying tongue,*
> *Hands that shed innocent blood,*
> *A heart that devises wicked plans,*
> *Feet that make haste to run to evil,*
> *A false witness who breathes out lies*
> *And one who sows discord among brothers.*

God is the truth. His words are the truth, and I believe that any time I'm suggesting, assuming, or inferring what may not be true, I'm lying, and I'm bearing false witness against my neighbor. When I read these words in Proverbs again, I noticed that five of the seven things that the Lord hates and finds detestable clearly speak of lying, gossiping, and seeking to create conflict. In other words, it's a big deal to the Lord to do these things—so much so that he made it a Commandment.

My opinion on this Commandment is that for most of us, it doesn't seem as severe as the others. Imagine how often we engage in chatter about someone else's life, even if we don't mean harm. "An evildoer listens to wicked lips, and a liar gives ear to a mischievous tongue" (Proverbs 17:4). If we slander a person, we can be sued and potentially pay a large monetary fine. If we are in a courtroom, we must swear to tell the truth under oath or risk penalty of perjury, which could lead to jail. So why wouldn't we take all forms of bearing false witness a little more seriously outside of a courtroom?

Could it be because we've not faced judgment? The judgment and consequences we face when there's a crime we deem more serious like stealing, likely gives us pause before doing it. What consequence would it take for us not to bear false witness? God spoke through Moses making it clear He didn't want us to commit this breach in the rules, so why do we do it anyway and often without forethought? "You shall not go around as a slanderer among your people, and you shall not stand up against the life of your neighbor: I am the Lord" (Leviticus 19:16).

Do you remember being on the elementary school playground chanting, "Sticks and stones may break my bones, but words will never hurt me"? Whoever came up with that possibly meant well, but in hindsight it sounds like saying it's all right to assault me, go ahead, but whatever you're saying doesn't hurt me. In fact, it does hurt (and so would any blow to the bones).

I can still vividly recall a scene on the playground and the third-grade boy teasing me because of my name. I bet you can guess it. A popular jingle in the seventies was his ammo. "When you've got Libby's, Libby's, Libby's on the label, label, label, you will like it, like it, like it on your table, table, table." Of course I was so embarrassed and it did hurt my feelings, so I retaliated with a few rhyming words of my own. I'll just say his name rhymes with heart and you can guess the word I used to tease him right back. It was self-defense as far as I was concerned, and I did my darnedest to defend my position but the playground monitor didn't hear what he said, so I was the only one that got in trouble at recess. Not fair! I was humiliated and punished all in one day.

This was a pretty tame experience all things considered, but it has obviously stuck with me all these years later.

What soul damaging words have we used towards people in innocence? Or with intent? To say the tongue is a mightier than the sword is evident not only by how we've been hurt by words, but also by what's written in scriptures.

I tell you, on the day of judgment people will give account for every careless word they speak (Matthew 12:36).

A gentle tongue is a tree of life but perverseness in it breaks the spirit (Proverbs 15:4).

Keep your tongue from evil and your lips from speaking deceit (Psalm 34:13).

If anyone thinks he is religious and does not bridle his tongue but deceives his heart, this person's religion is worthless (James 1:26).

Let no corrupting talk come out of your mouths, but only such as is good for building up, as fits the occasion, that it may give grace to those who hear (Ephesians 4:29).

We must recognize that our words can cause pain. In my opinion there's a real problem in our world of bullying. When I was growing up, this didn't seem nearly as prevalent as it is today, at least not that I remember. There were the occasional situations, but they were definitely few and far between. The offender would suffer immediate consequences from teachers or parents, and ultimately, bullies were set straight. Zero to low tolerance was the modus operandi back in the seventies. Moving the guardrails of tolerance coupled with prevalence in social media I suspect have played a part in the delivery of such harmful tactics today, but at some point we just need to know it's wrong and not allow this behavior to continue.

The root of name-calling, speaking lies, gossiping, and creating havoc on a person could simply be a form of insecurity, jealousy, pain, and circumstances that can be hard to imagine. That said, it goes back to a matter of the heart, and if our hearts are filled with brokenness, it's probable we pass it on ("hurting people hurt people"). I'm working to have compassion for the word slayers and try looking for the "why" in their efforts to hurt others.

Realizing bullies come in all sizes, I sadly observe that some grow up to become bigger, older, and more intimidating. They can even have influence over our children and if we aren't strong in our convictions, they will influence us too. Do we allow those with influence permission to speak to our children in ways we would never speak to them? Words used can be damaging or they can be uplifting and powerful in a positive way. The question is what are we willing to do to protect this type of emotional abuse toward our children and ourselves? Matthew 12:34–35 says, "Out of the abundance of the heart the mouth speaks. The good person out of his good treasure brings forth good, and the evil person out of his evil treasure brings forth evil."

I raised my children in a wonderful community in Dallas, Texas. Making lifelong friends, I experienced some of my most treasured memories during that time. I can hardly recall a year when at least one of the kids wasn't involved in team sports. This world consumed our family for a season of time, which still resonates with many special experiences and friendships. Within those experiences, however, some were less positive. There were parents (I may have been one of these parents at times) who paid attention to what rules applied to certain athletes and what rules were bent. Who was subjected to more criticism, and who received a pass? Emotions were plenty, largely due to inconsistencies in expectations, and this brought out the least attractive sides of coaches, parents, spectators, and athletes. It appeared subjective decisions were part of the culture, and you could accept this or be an island, so to speak. I leaned toward being an island but still wanted to know what was happening on the mainland.

Causing difficulty for others takes on countless forms and is sinful according to God's Word. Harsh words, gossiping, and teaching falsehoods count too. I struggle to wrap my head around the intentions of spreading falsehoods for sport, but then my heart opens to the possibility that not everything is always as it seems. Yes, there is just plain mean, but I tend to believe the best in people rather than defaulting to question ulterior motives. Praying for these people is our best defense—praying for hearts to be broken for the Lord and opened to His love and grace.

Extending grace and being open to a perspective that's different from ours are examples of how having compassion is more important than always going by the proverbial book. Keeping score or tabs on our friends, teammates, classmates, colleagues, or family can occupy our minds and hearts beyond recognition of keeping God's commandments. So to follow the rules is good. To worry about how others are doing at it, not so much. Perhaps we leave the scorecard to God. "For all have sinned and fall short of the glory of God" (Romans 3:23).

Our pointed words aren't always meant for harm. I'm not a fan of jokes. Too many times to count, I've felt the brunt of jokes or "The joke's on me, not you," and my largest disdain comes from not delivering a joke well or not getting the joke at all. It's so awkward when someone is telling a joke, and I truly don't get it. I laugh and look around, wondering if I'm the only one not getting it, and what's wrong with me that I don't think it's funny. I've talked with Curt about this more than once, because he does like to tease. I know his heart is always in the right place where I'm concerned, and most people mean well for that matter, but does the joker always know that? Is it all right to joke around, speaking of our neighbor in a way we think is funny? Or do we need to know our audience to ensure we're all on the same page?

It's all funny until someone is embarrassed, uncomfortable, or, worse, offended. I hadn't considered joking to fall under God's Commandment of bearing false witness. Or does it? If we're creating difficulty for them that could be stirring up emotions or bad memories, maybe we aren't aware, but we could be hurting someone, unlocking a trigger. The hope is that we all understand who's listening, but when faced with the possibility of our language causing difficulty for anyone, it's best to think twice.

I do however love a good anecdote. Stories are funnier with the added twists and turns and amplified expressions. Does this classify as sin if we're just having fun with a tale? "Tall" or not? There are likely generations of false information we've passed down by teaching what isn't true. "If you swallow seeds, they will grow in your stomach," "Step on a crack, break your mother's back," or my all-time favorite "Ricky Bobby" quote: "If you're not first, you're last." With perfect timing, Walker actually got me laughing hysterically with this one, and I'll never forget it!

Are we sinning when we tell these tales? Is it up to God to decide? Or is it based on our intentions when we tell them? I can't help but think about a salesman attempting a sale to an innocent prospect. Whether it's stocks, cars, food, services, or "fill in the blank," how far are we willing to go to deceive for our gain? This lying, wicked scheming is sin, and I doubt any of us really intentionally are up to such tricks. But we might know someone who is comfortable for the sake of a dollar, with a no-harm-no-foul mindset, willing to mislead, misspeak, or misguide. As followers of Christ, how can we effect change in others? Perhaps claiming the Commandment as important to keep is a good start! It's important we remember that as Christians, we are called to expand God's kingdom. Our words and actions are noticed by our neighbors, so being who we say we are isn't a switch to turn on and off.

> "The greatest single cause of atheism in the world today is Christians, who acknowledge Jesus with their lips and walk out the door, and deny Him by their lifestyle. That is what an unbelieving world simply finds unbelievable." —Brennan Manning

As we attempt to teach the Bible, God's Word, and disciple others, I'm inclined to believe we need to have our information straight. Be certain we are clear on what we're teaching. For example, if a man is pounding his chest while yelling at his wife, "Obey me; the Bible says so," is this what God means in Ephesians when he says that the woman is to obey her husband? As students of His Word, teaching falsehoods isn't likely our plan, but if we aren't thoughtful about how and what we are saying, we could be skirting the line of truth, if not crossing it.

Lying is rooted in Satan from the Garden of Eden. Lying is murder with our tongues. Lying is based in deceit, and as I was always taught, the truth always comes out, so why lie? There may be reasons we feel led to lie about our own actions or even believe it's for a good reason. An example could be to protect someone we love or if we believe we are somehow doing God's will. This is a bit murky to me, because I'm certain I've lied to protect the innocent, but this still feels in the category of what God hates. If we do participate in this behavior, maybe we don't realize it or believe it's harmless. Maybe we get something out of it in an unhealthy way like wanting the subjects of our sin to hurt too. Curt says, "Misery loves company," and I believe he's onto something. Again- hurting people hurt people. This perspective has softened my heart for both the offender and the target.

I would say that bearing false witness against our neighbor is a misused commandment and one on the buffet line easier to skip over as important. Ellie made an interesting point: some people may feel they can't keep the Commandments, so why even try? To some it can be overwhelming, so they succumb to realizing we're going to break them; it's just a matter of when and figure it's not that big a deal. If we relate breaking commandments to our choices at a buffet, then it's not hard to understand why we can sometimes give up trying to make better choices with the tempting options staring us in the face. If my friends are piling on the savory fried options, breads, and several delicious desserts, it makes it harder to pick the healthy salad, skip the bread, and miss out on the juicy stuff. In other words, if I'm in a situation where people are gossiping, it can be hard to resist joining in either silently or aloud.

Having obedience and consistency in our daily consumption will parlay our intentions into good or bad results, depending on what we're consistently consuming. One way I approach positive results is by graciously verbalizing when I don't support gossip. Once I realized standing up for God's Commandment against bearing false witness was the truth, and the truth was not debatable, I became more confident in lovingly changing the narrative. I've found that not only does it feel good, but also on the occasions I begin going down the gossip road, the Holy Spirit quickly convicts me to stop.

Because I'm still on this journey too, the enemy has been attempting not only to distract me, but he actually successfully wooed me into bearing false witness against my neighbor multiple times recently—at least three that I can think of! I've been so distracted by life and things of the world that my priorities have shifted out of order. In my frustration, I finally remembered to pray for perspective! Too many times I've found myself spiraling and feeling out of sync and forgetting to lean on God for guidance. Once I did pray, the answer almost instantly came to me: the devil has been trying to keep me from being obedient to God's call for me. In doing so, he's had me running around, doing anything and everything besides what the Lord has asked of me. Dang devil!

But in God's divine way, *He* is always at least one step ahead of the enemy and knew he would attempt to take me off course. So instead of the enemy succeeding, God has nudged me to use this situation as an example of not only how easy it is to be tempted to turn our eyes away from God, but also to share how God has used this time to teach and remind me what it feels like to bear false witness. "And we know that for those who love God all things work together for good, for those who are called according to his purpose" (Romans 8:28).

In each of the three times I recall it happening, I knew immediately it was wrong, and I didn't like how it felt. What's interesting is that in each of these circumstances, I wasn't blatantly lying, but my actions were still bearing false witness. In one instance, I was suspicious of a person's intentions, so I inserted my opinion of what they could have been ... bearing false witness! In the second I allowed my pride and prior pain of not feeling valued dictate my emotions and cloud my perspective of a loved one's intent ... bearing false witness! In the third I inserted my very strong, unverified two cents toward a notorious family in not the kindest tone ... bearing false witness!

Fortunately, I had only shared these three known sins with Curt, so I was spared public scrutiny. But it might as well have been in public because it didn't feel so good experiencing the Holy

Spirit bubble up inside me or hearing the truth from my husband. The closer we are in our journey with the Lord, the more likely the enemy will try to attack us. But remember, God is a step ahead, and He has now helped me reconcile the hectic week as a lesson for my nourishment. Amen!

The Lord satisfies our appetites if we allow Him to serve us with what will fill us. In our attempts to have a buffet-style religion and relationship with God, we may not always select what's best for us, but He will. The opposite of bearing false witness against our neighbor is to serve them with kindness. Serving others is intended to grow us while we're contributing to the kingdom. The theme of knowing our hearts applies in service too. When we are serving to advance the kingdom and feel compelled to do so, it likely will provide fulfillment for us. How we feed others comes with a responsibility and awareness to pay attention to what we serve and how.

In complete honesty, there have been situations where I was checking a box, getting my "drive through" meal deal to satisfy what needed filling. It was more comfortable hand-selecting my level of commitment to do what was expected. We aren't all designed to serve and give the same way. In the body of Christ, we each have a specific function and for me it isn't always serving Him the same way as my neighbor. I used to be bothered by this thought wondering what was wrong with me when I didn't feel inclined to build a house for the homeless or deliver food to the infirm, although it absolutely mattered to me. If we are all to raise money or plan a fundraiser for a cause, who would read to a child after school who needs extra help? If we all served at soup kitchens feeding the hungry, who would deliver supplies to the sick? If we all wrote a check for our favorite cause, who would volunteer for the cause?

I found myself serving where I didn't feel as good about it

as I believed others felt, and I continued to wonder what was wrong with me. Was I serving for the wrong reasons? This wasn't what I wanted. Matthew 6:1 says, "Beware of practicing your righteousness before other people in order to be seen by them, for then you will have no reward from your Father who is in heaven."

I had more than one conversation about this with Curt and have always respected and admired his desire to serve the hungry. It's a calling for him to donate food and contribute to our community by supporting this need. So why wasn't it my call to do the same? I felt more inclined to serve and give elsewhere. My heart pulled me in a different direction but I would ask myself if this role was as important. "Just as the body is one and has many members, and all the members of the body, though many are one body, so it is with Christ. ... For the body does not consist of one member but of many. If the foot should say, 'Because I am not a hand, I do not belong to the body,' that would not make it any less a part of the body" (1 Corinthians 12:12, 14–15). And just like that it clicked. I am a different part of the body that serves according to the gifts God has given me. My gifts, my purpose, and my calling are placed in me by the Holy Spirit for His glory. You have unique gifts intended for His glory too, so lean into that understanding. I found that what I naturally enjoy and believe I do well is how I am to serve Him. Coincidence?

So often we fill our lives doing service, volunteering, signing up for this commitment or that cause all in the name of service, but it may also be to fill a void where something is missing. It's up to us to figure that out. In my case, I was missing the fullest love my heavenly Father had in store for me. Looking everywhere but to Him for my cup to run over, I was finally exhausted.

I spent many years serving, full well knowing in my deepest core I was serving for affirmation. The source of affirmation was there all along. While I was busy looking around at everyone else's buffet plates and overloading my buffet plates, instead I would have been better served by seeking God to fill my cup and load my plate and praying how He wanted me to serve Him and my neighbors.

It's important that we share what's on our plates and serve those serving us as well. This is a wonderful way to disciple. Where I got it wrong was acting often alone. I needed God, we all do, and it wasn't until I allowed Him to "carry my tray" that I found the ultimate affirmation. He filled my cup.

Most of us are familiar with the sisters Mary and Martha and how they acted differently towards Jesus. Martha was busy making sure everything was just as it was supposed to be in the house. A guest was coming so she was preparing and serving Him. Mary, however, was focused on the guest, Jesus, and what He was saying. So often we can become so busy doing what we think needs to be done to please God that we forget to talk with Him, listen to Him, and be in relationship with Him. When we serve, we might take notice if we're serving for Him or for us. Should it be both? I believe the answer is yes, it should be both.

Some people come to know Christ through serving, and it's possibly a more comfortable path for them. God wants us to be in relationship with people, and He designed us to be in community, not alone. Spending time focusing on our relationship with God is critical, but we mustn't forget the other critical piece of His will for us: loving our neighbors. The Ten Commandments encourage us to participate in both our relationship with God and people, although we may not all get to this place in the same way. Remembering that when we open ourselves up to both relationships, we will experience the fulfillment of having our cake and eating it too, in a healthy way!

Underestimating the weight of the Ten Commandments may result in our never being fully satisfied. It's possible we're misusing the Ten Commandments by not using them enough. The enemy is at work trying to desensitize us to sin. Temptation is all around us, and the attempts to skew our minds have reached the point where we can become unfazed by certain sin. To bear false witness against our neighbor is wrong, but it is forgivable, and the Holy Spirit will continue to nudge us toward more nourishing actions. Acknowledging that all sin is relevant to God, I'm encouraging us to take inventory of our habits, preconceptions, and hearts and recognize that God loves us and that He wrote the Ten Commandments to protect us and be in relationship with us. I've gone from seeing my relationship with God as private; to full-out "you know what I believe." Reclaiming the relevance of God's Commandments has strengthened my relationship with Him, and I am certain it will do the same for you. Loading up at His buffet table is a built-in feast, always satisfying and open twenty-four hours a day!

WHAT ARE YOUR THOUGHTS?

1) What part of bearing false witness against your neighbor do you struggle with most? Gossiping, teaching what isn't true, creating conflict, sharing what isn't your story to share, or something else?

_____

_____

_____

_____

2) Has your relationship with God felt like a religious buffet at times? How?

_____

_____

_____

_____

3) Which Commandments are you more likely to justify?

_____

_____

_____

_____

4) Is it easier for you to serve or be served? Why?

_____

_____

_____

_____

FIVE

RISKY BUSINESS

Therefore do not be foolish, but understand what the
will of the Lord is.

—Ephesians 5:17

Are there risks of not following the Ten Commandments? The majority opinions from people I've asked say yes, there are risks, but they aren't fully clear on them all and whether they are numerous or few. To take a risk means to expose to hazard or danger or to face potential loss or injury. So how does this apply to following the Ten Commandments, or does it? My opinion is simply that we face the potential loss of ultimate abundance and a deeper relationship with God; this is the gamble we make if we take the risk of not abiding in the Ten Commandments.

The 1980s movie *Risky Business*, in case you missed it, is iconic and filled with a lot of adventurous antics from the main character, Joel, while his parents are out of town. There's a famous scene where he slides across the floor in his socks, not wearing much besides his smile and sunglasses. Dancing and singing his heart out like a Cheshire cat stuffed with pride, he's living it up, until (spoiler alert) he gets caught. It's always fun living on the edge until someone gets exposed or hurt. This is a basic truth my mom taught me at a young age. "Stop roughhousing and playing chase in the house! Someone is going to get hurt!" And someone always did; just ask my brother Randy. That's the thing about taking risks, there's a risk of it not working, not panning out, not being such a good idea after all, and in some cases there's risk of serious consequences. Like the protagonist in the movie, are we playing roulette with sin, and if so are the risks worth the consequences?

It's not worth it to me, yet I risk consequences daily. Not necessarily knowingly, but undoubtedly I do. The difference between knowingly taking risks and not knowing is that when we consciously weigh the consequences against the presumed need to take the risk, we can most likely accept the consequence. If we jaywalk, most often we won't get a citation. If we speed, we may or may not get pulled over and receive a ticket. If we cheat on a test, we could be caught and fail.

If we knowingly walk into a situation that is dangerous and risk our safety, this is foolish. We make decisions based on consequences and willingness to take the risks every day. If we look at the consequences of sin, some seem minor in the world, but are they minor to God? What is minor to some may be major to another, but are there any minor infractions in God's eyes, or does He grade us on a sliding sin scale if He grades us at all?

There are those of us who can break them without awareness of our sin and at other times break them feeling like it's not a big deal—no harm, no foul. Believing God will forgive if we ask Him to be forgiven could be skewed as, although it's true, a risky perspective on sin. I wonder: if our forgiveness were dependent on our level of remorse, would we engage in taking risks with His Commandments? Because of what Jesus did for us on the cross, we are offered God's grace.

My friend Tim shared his story of a job he wanted many years ago. He prayed about the position and really felt God telling him not to take it. But Tim really wanted to take the job. He told me that he could clearly hear the Lord tell him, "Yeah, you can take the job, but it will cost you. You'll have consequences in your marriage, and you'll turn your hobby into a chore that will no longer be your passion." It was up to Tim to weigh these risks and consequences doing what he wanted for worldly gain versus abiding in what God wanted for him. Tim didn't know then how God was preparing him and had better plans for him professionally and personally. Tim didn't take the job and still has his hobby and passion fully intact, I'm delighted to report.

It's important to note that while risking God's plans for his own, if Tim had taken the position, he would have blatantly lauded himself before honoring the Lord and therefore worshipped himself before God. "You shall have no other gods before me" (Exodus 20:3). Loving myself first is a daily struggle I oftentimes overlook for some reason. If you have that same struggle, acknowledging that breaking the commandments in some fashion every day is real, do you consider it may have to do with consequences? Few or no apparent consequences could still be yet to come. It's possible that there's a compound effect for consequences, and if we turn a blind eye to what's building up over years of taking risks, they may manifest when and how we least expect it.

I'm not a fan of speculating and assuming, although I default to this way of thinking much too often. When it comes to taking risks with certain sins, I have 100 percent made poor decisions with little thought of consequences or speculating they wouldn't be severe and therefore worth the risk. *Yikes!* What kind of thinking is this? If consequences were more severe like they are for some laws in the world like stealing or murder, they would likely warrant more forethought. Taking these risks could mean jail or worse and would be life-altering, heartbreaking, and costly. If we treated all sin with caution, taking certain risks might not be so seemingly prevalent.

Imagine if after using the name of the Lord in vain, we were met with a sudden fear of being exposed. What if our neighbor heard us and had the option to turn us in to the police for this infraction? If the penalty were to pay a fine, like a parking ticket, would we think twice before selecting our words? This example applies to all of the Ten Commandments actually, and aren't we fortunate that there's no citation neighbors can issue for the misappropriation of a Sabbath each week.

If we spent even one day focused on the risks and consequences of all Ten Commandments, my prediction is our reverence for them would increase exponentially. Flipping the script to see from a different point of view offers encouragement to hold His Commandments near as still relevant. By rediscovering His Commandments, I've found the beauty in store for us, the blessings available, and the reality that no risk I take is worth the consequence I feel when I sin, whether knowingly or unknowingly.

I love the liturgical confession of sin in the Episcopal Book of Common Prayer that asks God to please forgive us all our sins, "known and unknown." It's resonated with me that I sin without knowing it. I'm grateful for that blanket forgiveness nonetheless, but how often *are* we sinning and consciously not aware of it? I'm betting, a lot! Is this because we have underscored certain commandments as really bad and therefore neglect to consider the gravity of all the others? So often we get into a rhythm of how we think, and as with any pattern, we need to shift our thinking; just a little will make a difference. But in the meantime like so many people, I've skirted the lines of sin a little too close in the past and crossed them. Since writing and studying more about the Ten Commandments, I've become more aware when I get close to or cross the sin line, but it still happens. Talk about feeling compelled by the Holy Spirit! It's up to us to pay closer attention to when we break a commandment and why. From personal experience, I'm much more aware of my actions and intentions when attempting to *live His commandments.*

We've established that the risk of harsh consequences causes most of us to steer clear of breaking laws and commandments like murder and stealing. The layers of stealing leave me wondering however, if I'm unknowingly stealing. We may not rob a bank or take a knickknack from our neighbor's living room, but what if we grab a bottle of water from their fridge without asking, sample a chocolate from the bulk bins at the grocery store, or steal time from a friend or colleague? What about stealing dreams, credit, or ideas? Are those still considered stealing? If this is what God means by "You shall not steal," it's debatable that stealing isn't so cut-and-dried as we may have believed.

About fifteen years ago, a young boy about ten years old spent hours creating an idea for a new sports team. He created the name, the mascot, the colors and the uniforms. Drawing as neatly as a young boy could and coloring in the uniform design on printer copy paper, he labored for many days at his family's dining room table. Excited to share the idea with one he thought was a trusted friend and professional in the industry, he laid out his idea with his parents' proud consent. He was met with enthusiasm from the pro and the excitement to move forward began.

Or so they all thought. Within a few weeks his parents picked up a flyer at a nearby school announcing the development of a new sports organization in the community. To the shock of them all, the name, colors, and mascot were exactly the same as their son's.

The "trusted" friend and industry professional hadn't kept the idea confidential and had shared it with another friend. It wasn't clear if that was an unintentional error in judgment or part of a greater scheme, but the benefit of the doubt was extended. In the end, the young boy's idea was stolen, as were his time, his excitement, and his dream. If your blood is starting to boil, I think this would be considered righteous anger and fine by me.

His parents were outraged, appalled, and hurt, confused, sad, and let down among many more adjectives. If they felt all of these emotions, they felt even more strongly over their son's injustice. How could someone steal his dream? His idea? Where was the justice? I'll tell you where: in knowing the Lord would deal with it. As difficult as all of this was in the moment, the opportunity to teach a greater lesson had manifested. There could have been some name-calling and retaliation, but they ultimately dealt with the situation with grace and the wisdom that God was protecting their son somehow. As hard as that is at any age to grasp, God is looking out for us and protecting us every day. We never quite know how He protects us in the moment, but even when others persecute us, treat us unfairly, or perhaps steal from us, these difficult situations can be used for good. Still, it's challenging to realize it in the circumstance.

Reflecting on this experience led me to check myself, trying to recall an instance where I may have unintentionally stolen. A memory came to mind of a lesson taught by my amazing mom. I was probably around six or seven when Randy and I had been to the Heights Variety Store in our neighborhood. These were the good old days when the local merchant knew all of his customers and their children. You could buy almost anything there, from school supplies to costumes, crafts, games, and candy. This was nearly fifty years ago, so some details escape me, but the gist is that I took a couple pieces of candy from the store without paying for them.

When we got home, I innocently told my mom that I had picked up a few pieces of candy, and she was instantly stunned and disappointed in me. I remember being stunned too and upset that I had done something wrong. How did I know I wasn't allowed to take the candy? I surely wouldn't have taken it or offered up this intel had I known my mom's reaction. After all, there were several open buckets of candy just inviting me to take some. I didn't see a sign that said I had to buy it, so I thought it must be free.

My mom made me go back to the store and tell the owner what I had done. She explained to me this was stealing even if I didn't mean to do it and even if the owner would likely never know. It was wrong; it was stealing, and God would know. The store owner was kind and graciously forgave me. I believe he may have given me the candy after all, knowing I was embarrassed, a good little girl who didn't mean to steal.

What liberties do we take that we may not consider a big deal when it comes to keeping our hand out of the cookie jar? What about keeping the change after running an errand for Mom? It's Mom, and she wouldn't mind. As a matter of fact, if we asked her for a dollar, she would probably give it to us, so knowing that she would give it to us anyway should make it all right to go ahead and take it. Wouldn't it? What about taking a bite off my husband's plate without asking? Am I *really* stealing? This doesn't count, right? We all know the old saying that what's his is mine, so I can eat off my husband's plate because technically it's mine and we're one. Hey, this logic works, right?

What about realizing I wasn't charged for a grocery item that made it home with me? Is this my fault because I didn't catch it at the store? If I unknowingly stole an avocado, is it a sin? Maybe it falls under the philosophy that it all evens out in the wash, because there are plenty of times I've paid for groceries when an item didn't make it into my bag. The list of possibilities to justify is endless, and these are seemingly the "little thefts" to question. We could probably all agree that taking what doesn't belong to us is stealing, but are there gray areas or exceptions to the rules on stealing? If so, by what authority do we decide if it's all right and in which situations?

I think about a scenario all too real where there are hungry children around the world. If their parents are suffering and have no money, is it all right for them to steal food for survival? Surely God would understand and not be upset, because this is an extenuating circumstance. This is a question that puzzles me, because my heart says it would be okay, but is it still stealing and breaking one of God's commandments? This falls on the list of questions I would like to ask God when I get to heaven. Could we have a little clarity on extenuating circumstances for stealing and any other sins that may confuse us? I'm looking for loopholes, potentially, but with good reasons. My go-to approach is praying that God knows our hearts, loves us for who we are in all circumstances, including the confusion, and will grant us needed wisdom in response to our questions.

All these questions have value, and we may not know the answers clearly until we see our Father in heaven, but it provokes thought for me to pause. Pause before I assume it's okay to interrupt someone and steal their time, or pause before I steal the last french fry or the last bite of pie from my husband's plate. Because I know how much he loves me, he probably wouldn't care and would want me to have it anyway, but it's the thought that counts. I shouldn't take without asking. We need to always be thoughtful of our actions when taking is involved; it may very well be stealing. The arrogance of attitude combined with some of the entitlement running rampant these days in our society offers us all the opportunity to pause and ask ourselves if we deserve what we're taking. Is it ours to take, and are we risking consequences? Is it really stealing? What other sin risks might we be taking if we've not considered all sides of stealing as sin?

I've said that calling ourselves Christians if we aren't walking with Him is risking the use of saying the Lord's name in vain. I'm not saying we aren't Christians; Jesus came to save us, and that's undeniable. What I mean, however, is that if we're not walking the walk we talk, we risk stealing an opportunity to bring someone closer to Christ. Our senior pastor, Scot Longyear, gave an example of this in a recent sermon. He poignantly described that if we act one way on Saturday night in front of our peers but are "acting" like followers of Christ in worship on Sunday morning, how does this affect those around us on Saturday night? Could it be that we're posing as Christians and confusing those around us? What if we are the reason for discouraging people from following Christ?

In other words, because we aren't authentic in our intents, we create confusion and delegitimize what it means to be a Christian. So in essence, instead of bringing people one step closer to Christ, we might be moving them away from following Him at all. I would not want to be responsible for this particular theft or a participant in observing it either, but have I been without knowing it? God can choose to use us for His purposes in bringing someone closer to Him. We may have a small part to play in planting seeds, so being alert to knowing this is important.

Naysayers of Christianity have a tendency to point out how bad Christians are at following the commandments. We don't always act like the Ten Commandments exist, and in particular they can be used to exploit others' shortcomings and faults versus encouraging the mercy God has shown us by creating them. These same naysayers also attempt to discredit us with finger-pointing and name-calling such as "hypocrite" and "liar." What amuses me, however, is that God isn't fooled by these accusations, and neither are His followers.

Now, in saying this, I do believe we can use these moments to call into question how we're doing as followers. Have we asked God to forgive us? Are we working to grow closer to God, and are we growing in our efforts at walking the walk? Are we busy pointing out the sins of others, at the risk of not recognizing our own sins? It's important not to ignore the risks of hypocrisy and consequences when calling ourselves Christians, but most importantly, we don't want to risk not bringing people closer to God's kingdom. Matthew 28:19 says, "Go therefore and make disciples of all nations, baptizing them in the name of the Father, and of the son and of the Holy Spirit." Matthew 4:19 says, "Follow me, and I will make you fishers of men."

We are the church, and God asks us to bring people to Him. If we aren't modeling what knowing Him looks like, not only are we at risk of missing out on knowing God's joy and abundance, but in a sense, we're stealing that opportunity from our neighbors by not sharing it with them. Encouraging them to experience what we have received is what we're called to do. How we're doing in this call is for us to discern.

I wonder: if we aren't doing as God asks of us, are we in essence butting heads with God? Working against Him? I don't believe He needs us to make anything happen, but I do believe He wants us to be part of the formula so we can experience the joy in seeing the kingdom grow.

As I listened to author, speaker, and podcaster Gabe Lyons speak on this subject, something he said really struck me. He said that two out of five Americans believe "people of faith" (42 percent) and "religion" (46 percent) are part of the problem Christianity is increasingly being labeled as irrelevant and extreme in our society. The gospel story has been distorted over the last century in a way that had withstood the test of time for over two thousand years. How has the happened, and what can we do about it? The enemy has certainly created chaos to take full advantage of distorting the truth of what it is to be a Christian. What we can do is remember we're partnering with God to be disciples of His story. Don't stop talking about Him, and don't be afraid to tell the gospel story, including on Saturday night!

As we share the gospel, we may be met with resistance and some questioning the relevance of God and the Ten Commandments. We need to be armed with knowledge as to why they are absolutely still relevant. Additionally, we need to walk in humility when we sin, because we will still sin. Being transparent is critical to accomplish these goals. If you've had an opportunity to share your testimony, you'll likely agree it's been a true blessing—not just for the person you're sharing it with, but also for you. Being part of the team to foster hope in a friend's suffering marriage or offering a story of real-life redemption and abundance can be literally awesome and life-changing. Not only are you honoring God in the process and giving Him the credit and glory for the goodness in your life, but also you can see the hope in the eyes of the person you want to bring closer to Christ. This is why it's important to share our stories and also why it's important when we fall, to be humble and let those around us, who are not as close to Christ, see what humility, hope, and grace look like. The risks of keeping our sin struggles a secret are plenty, but among the greatest risks is robbing us of freedom in forgiveness and stealing the opportunity to be a kingdom builder. I second author Ann Voskamp who said, "God can only get all the glory when I tell the whole story."

Part of this journey is to better understand what the Ten Commandments mean and how we may have underestimated our need for them. If we believe they're still relevant, then I propose we invest energy into following them. I don't believe we need to become legalistic about following them, because our growth and our relationship with Jesus aren't dependent on rules. Jesus made that sacrifice for us, but what I do believe is we will have a richer relationship with God and an abundant life from obedience to His Commandments.

Whether we're pressed or not by a nonbeliever to explain

them or justify our need for them, we have an opportunity and responsibility to be more educated on the subject for our growth. Just as with anything we're interested in, from gardening and cooking to playing golf or hunting, we spend time researching what's necessary to be proficient in that area or risk being unprepared.

My husband is a hunter and spends time each year preparing for the next hunting season. He spends time sharpening his skills and knowledge, even though he's been hunting for more than forty years. For Curt to say, "I'm a hunter," and then not want to gain more knowledge and experiences to make him a better hunter could limit his growth as a sportsman. Each year I watch him sight in his weapons, conduct target practice with his bow, study the weather patterns, read related articles and have conversations with fellow hunters to strengthen his knowledge of his passion. The same applies to growing the church and growing our knowledge of God and His commands. When we spend time in continuing education of our Christian faith, not only will we become more prepared to bring others to know Him, but it will open our eyes to those around us seeking to know the Lord.

It's been illuminating to discover how relevant the Ten Commandments truly are in our culture. Feeling judged for my sin, knowing my accusers were also sinners, kick-started my curiosity and desire for growth in understanding more about my sin, the sin nature of others, and the relevance of God's Commandments. Should we be challenged with the perspective that they don't apply anymore or they're not relevant, let's be prepared to rebut and defend what God wrote in stone, which is significant. It means that it's an absolute. Someone can say they don't believe the content of the Commandments, but they can't deny they exist.

Many believers and nonbelievers find the Ten Commandments

a passé idea. They're not seen as necessarily practical today and have been deconstructed like traditional courtship or Victorian manners. I'm all about manners, protocol, and old-fashioned courtship, so in my opinion, some things aren't meant to change. Manners of past decades and eras and many other traditions that have been relaxed and treated as passé may be making a comeback. I'm for the Ten Commandments' comeback!—not just that they come in handy and don't seem so antiquated anymore, but that they are seen as consistently applicable. When we call someone out on stealing, why does it matter, or how do we know it's wrong if there's not a foundation for this being wrong? We can't have it both ways.

Believers and nonbelievers alike, can't ignore the gravity of the Ten Commandments on the one hand, yet pull them out to support their belief that something is wrong when it suits them to justify a position, opinion, or circumstance. Likewise, the relevance of the Ten Commandments doesn't stop when the New Testament begins, so the argument by some to negate our need for them doesn't hold water to me. I believe the New Testament was written to support and fulfill what was written in the Old Testament. Following them or not doesn't get us into heaven, but acknowledging Jesus as our Savior, acknowledging His Word, and asking forgiveness when we sin *is* a pathway to a right relationship with Him. We gain the fullness of the life God wills for us when we follow the Ten Commandments, which is obedience to God.

It's helpful if we have tools that hold us accountable, just as with any good practice in life. If we look at the Commandments as the "check engine light," we can examine our hearts to realize if we even want to "look under the hood." Often, we would rather ignore the warning light than deal with the problem—or even disconnect the wires, so to speak, in order to avoid being reminded of potential underlying risks. The cool thing about paying attention to the "check engine" light is that if we are genuine about our desire to grow in our faith, we have a built-in Guide to help us along the way, the Holy Spirit.

Friends of mine, Scott and his wife Carmen, have a podcast and blog called "Your Everyday Life." I was reading their blog the other day, and Scott wrote about this very idea:

> This reminds me of how God operated in the Old Testament. He was that beacon of light shining down from above, and many times shining His light through Prophets to guide His people. Now Jesus has brought God down to our everyday lives, alive through His Spirit in us. He used to be out on the rock (His foundation) as a lighthouse, showing the way. Now it is a high-tech onboard system, with Him living in us and guiding us from within and leading us in our every-day-walking-around-kind-of-life.

When I read what Scott said, it truly resonated with me that we all are searching for signs from God to help us make decisions. The answers are within embedded in His Word and us. They are there all the time; we simply need to tap into them. Knowing this helps me claim the Commandments' relevance all the more; otherwise, what is the Holy Spirit guiding us toward or away from?

While interviewing my children, I asked this relevance question, and they all three said, "Yes, they're still relevant." We need the Ten Commandments as our guide to instill order in our lives and to guide us to live our best possible experience within our lives. We need them to grow closer to God so that our life is joyful. Ellie added that we may not always think about them, but they're relevant because we know we can rely on them as we're trying to be obedient to God. They give us an anchor. Tim summarized my children's beliefs, adding they provide a framework for our moral compass and current laws keep them relevant in the world. They are the sin we need forgiveness from; they're why we need a Savior!

We depend on the New Testament for teaching about Jesus and God's grace. In certain denominations the liturgy and Eucharist underscore His grace, but have they become irrelevant to our culture? It would seem sometimes yes and many, many times over if looking at our screens, social media, communities, and schools are any indication. God, the church, money, integrity, deception, greed, virtue, power, manipulation, gossip, selfishness, lies, profanity, and jealousy—where and how do the Ten Commandments apply in our daily lives with all of these attitudes and influences? So much good in our world is oftentimes overshadowed by what we are conditioned to see, which is oftentimes beyond vile and inappropriate to see in my opinion. Much of my adult life I've wondered if our perspectives would be different if what we were seeing on the news, at the movies, and on social media was all positive and uplifting rather than negative or disturbing. Would we make different decisions or have a different approach regarding sin and the risks encompassing sin? What if there was a code of conduct we all agreed to follow, a.k.a. the Ten Commandments? Would attitudes be different? Do we tend to accept risking what we believe is a better choice for the louder norm?

All too often I hear how people believe they've been wronged. It's time for justice and retaliation. When we don't agree with circumstances, there are two paths we can choose, and sometimes it's challenging to make the right decision. If we were living in the days before Christ, retaliation was a daily norm, it seems to me. Scripture is filled with battles, maneuvers, attacks, and a lot of brutality. Recently I reread the Bible, and the Old Testament continues to upset me. All the evil and barbaric treatment of people turns my stomach. To live in a time of an eye for an eye and a tooth for a tooth wouldn't go over today, I have a feeling. Leviticus 24:19–20 says, "If anyone injures his neighbor, as he has done it shall be done to him, fracture for fracture, eye for eye, tooth for tooth; whatever injury he has given a person shall be given to him." Is this how we want to live? Maybe it would stop certain people in their sin tracks if they risked facing a literal eye gouging.

We all know of a circumstance when this type of retaliation happens; for instance, "He hit me, so I'm going to hit him," or "She hurt me, so I will hurt her." What if instead we all followed the words of Matthew 5:38–39, "You have heard that it was said 'An eye for an eye, and a tooth for a tooth.' But I say to you, Do not resist the one who is evil. But if anyone slaps you on the right cheek, turn to him the other also." Or Luke's significant words in chapter 6:31, "As you wish that others would do to you, do so to them." There are risks of retaliation. If someone steals from you or breaks your bones, will you steal from them or break their bones? What would this gain us, if anything? Alternatively, do we live by the New Testament and treat people with grace, mercy, and love as Jesus does? Remember the words in Romans 12:17–19: "Repay no one evil for evil, but give thought to do what is honorable in the sight of all. If possible, so far as it depends on you, live peaceably with all. Beloved, never avenge yourselves, but leave it to the wrath of God, for it is written, 'Vengeance is mine, I will repay, says the Lord.'"

As we invite the Holy Spirit into our hearts, the Lord starts to work on us. The next time we feel like taking a chance with sin and minimizing the Ten Commandments, consider the risks. It's risky to ignore them by hindering our relationship with God and our neighbor. Whether it's stealing property, money, someone's time, a dream, a moment, an opportunity, or a career, or breaking one of God's other Commandments, they all come with a "be cautious of our steps" warning.

Knowing who we are and whose we are reminds us that God always has a plan for us, and I wouldn't want to be liable and risk diverting His plans. That said, what at times could seem unfair could be a blessing in disguise, so I'm learning not to risk being upset when I'm not clear on God's plans. God can make good of all things, so we are encouraged to pause in moments like these and look to God for clarity in confusing situations. He issues vengeance to those who wrong us, so our risk to retaliate against our offender or not forgive our brother could backfire, just as risking not bringing people closer to Him or underestimating how much we need the Ten Commandments could backfire. He has rescued me and restored my circumstances too many times to count. This is all the evidence I need not to knowingly take risks with sin and instead try and follow the Ten Commandments in order to experience God's blessings and a completely joyful, abundant life!

WHAT ARE YOUR THOUGHTS?

1) What risks have you taken with sin, either knowingly or unknowingly?

_____

_____

_____

_____

2) Do you believe all layers of stealing are sin? Are there situations when you've stolen with justification, e.g., time, ideas, a pencil from the office?

_____

_____

_____

_____

3) Do you believe you've taken risks by avoiding or interrupting bringing someone one step closer to Christ? If so, ask God whom He is calling you to disciple for His kingdom.

_____

_____

_____

_____

4) How do you see the Ten Commandments as still relevant, or do you?

_____

_____

_____

_____

SIX

WISE OLD OWLS

Listen to advice and accept instruction, that you
may gain wisdom in the future.

—Proverbs 19:20

I grew up in a time when there were things you simply didn't
do. Disrespecting your parents was one of them. The idea of
smarting off or challenging authority was without a doubt
met with raised eyebrows and definite consequences. Over the
years, I've observed a shift in the parent-child relationship. The
shift of children crossing that line of respect, which used to be
unthinkable, has become all too common. What happened? Or
am I misunderstanding this dynamic entirely? Did parents stop
demanding respect, or did children and younger generations lose
their guiding light? Could it be a combination of these, coupled
with the unwanted invitation of outside influences infiltrating our
families? Is it even the child who is to blame here, as we adults
tend to think?

Family dynamics can look a lot different today than the 1960s
and 70s childhood I experienced. Although not every family was
like mine, family still felt different to me then, especially the
sanctity of honor in the household. Has this shift affected the
dynamics of respect and honor in families? I love idyllic family
TV such as *Andy Griffith*, *Happy Days*, and *The Brady Bunch*,
which are often still airing today. It has to mean something that
they continue offering these programs. There must be enough

viewers interested in watching a more wholesome version of family life to keep them current and relatable fifty-plus years later. Do we long for those days, and do they still exist in some families? I do believe there are many households, Christian or not, that seek to have a dynamic with honor in the family. This is the value system I was raised with and the honor code children abided by over fifty years ago and certainly before. What happened to honor and respect in our nuclear families?

One fascinating article I read speaks on this very subject. It highlights that from generation to generation, children have pushed the boundaries of respect. This really isn't something new. It may seem worse, however, because children indeed face added changes and disruptions that weren't factors decades ago. The divide of the nuclear family, having one parent always at home versus outside childcare, disruptive forces like social media, and all-around apathy for education have most certainly contributed to the shift. Influences like entertainment and social media are bombarding our lives with images and messages lacking in filters, especially for our children, so no wonder I've noticed this shift, because there is one!

It spoke volumes to me when Ellie struggled with wanting her phone back after a two-week break from it while at camp each summer. Societal pressures and negative chatter from friends and the latest unvetted influencers were unwanted energy; although she knew she didn't want it, it was difficult to avoid. There was a thin line between not wanting to be bombarded with what was happening around her and FOMO (fear of missing out). After she had just spent two weeks filling her heart and soul with innocent fun and Jesus, she recognized how relaxed she had become and how something powerful was shifting in her: the reality of her world.

She wasn't ready to lose the peace she felt leaving camp.

Fortunately, we navigated her through these conflicting emotions. How do children navigate the confusing waters of this push-pull world if they don't have engaged, loving parents or parents at all? I wish I had all the answers, but these are just a few of the observations that have led me to question not only who and what influences our children, but our culpability in allowing it. In the moments of strength to effect change or set boundaries for a battle against "what everyone else is doing," another battle would break out under our roof! Ah, the joys of parenting!

My dad passed away when I was far too young to consider ever disrespecting him, so my sweet mother therefore received the brunt of all my emotions—his share and hers combined. I went through a short season of teenage snarkiness and rebellion. I look back and shudder when I think about this stretch of attitude, but at least I had been grounded in who I was and *whose* I was in order to find my way back to honoring my mother as she deserved. "Honor your father and your mother, that your days may be long in the land that the Lord your God is giving you" (Exodus 20:12).

My mom remained strong and resolved not to give up on me or slack off in her convictions to love me unconditionally and, when necessary, discipline me. She later shared her wisdom on raising children: "love and discipline." These two things go hand in hand. Love your children unconditionally, and sometimes that means there's discipline. You have to follow through on the consequences she insisted. So be sure you make the consequence such that you're not being punished too. Great advice!

When is the last time we disrespected one of our parents even as adults? Possibly we screened a call, raised our voice, rolled our eyes, spoke with condescension, or showed frustration toward our parents. Is this even what it means to honor our father and mother? Not only do I believe we aren't to disrespect our father and mother; I also believe how we represent our family name is critical. When my children, Dawson and Walker more specifically, are going on dates, are in a work environment, or wherever they are, I've stressed the point that they are representing the family name. In other words, "Honor me, and don't embarrass your dad, yourself, or me."

To honor means to regard or treat someone with admiration and respect. Why do you suppose God commanded us to admire and respect our father and mother? Could it be to save us from ourselves? Exodus 21:15, 17 reads, "Whoever strikes his father or his mother shall be put to death. ... Whoever curses his father or his mother shall be put to death." Yikes! This is a serious consequence for sure! But do you believe this punishment fits the crime here? If I'm being honest, I'm grateful that I have a Savior to forgive me of my sins, because otherwise, I would most definitely be dead by now several times over!

The amazing news, in addition to being forgiven for breaking this commandment as with all the others, is that this one commandment comes with a blessing.

My dear friend Liesl and I were talking a few years ago about parenting and our prayers for our children as they continued to grow in their faith. In our conversation, she was claiming this jewel of truth of God blessing us in this Commandment from the Lord. I remember in that moment feeling so fortunate, knowing we are able to receive this beautiful and wonderful gift. As many times as I had read the Ten Commandments, I hadn't fully digested the power in these words: "Honor your father and your mother, *that your days may be long in the land that the Lord your God is giving you*" (Exodus 20:12, emphasis added). This should be ample motivation for all of us to honor our parents. Even when we believe we are honoring them, do we truly honor them? Do we consciously honor them with a pure heart?

"If one curses his father or his mother, his lamp will be put out in utter darkness" (Proverbs 20:20). There are many scriptures related to honoring our parents, but there are also scriptures instructing us to honor God first. My view on this is that we need to allow the Holy Spirit to guide us, and while honoring our parents, we acknowledge God as the ultimate authority in our lives. Our parents are to be revered, respected, and honored, but that doesn't mean we have to always agree with them. My mom showed me an example of following God, and I want to always show my mom her value for giving me life, raising me, teaching me about God, providing for me, and loving me unconditionally. It's my goal to care for her needs in her older years and help her feel assured, respected, and loved.

My mom suffers from vascular dementia, and we are very grateful for my stepfather for loving her well during this season, but he needs our help and support too. Giving unconditional love and respect to our parents is what I believe it means to honor them—not only in private but also with our peers and family. I have not always extended the appropriate dose of honor that I'm called to give. This is an area I continue to examine, to ensure I'm truly abiding by God's Commandment. I'm not certain what blessings God intends for me, but my experience is that I've felt safe and loved from my mother and from God always. This feels like blessings!

Not everyone shares the gift of having such a devoted mother and parents. How do children receive blessings who don't have parents to honor? Does God grant equivalent blessings for abandoned children or those taken from dangerous parents? How can some children even contemplate honoring parents who have been abusive? What about stepparents? Are we required to apply honor to them? If children are raised by a relative, in foster care, or by an older sibling perhaps, are they to honor these people in the same way? And is there expiration on how long we have to continue honoring them, or is it in perpetuity?

Plain and simple, not every parent is a great parent! Not everyone parents the same, but one truth I can declare with certainty is that our Father God loves all His children well. Sadly, not all children have this experience from their earthly parents. In fact, their experience can be anywhere from intolerable and lacking to toxic, abusive, and horrific. I'm not qualified to know or say how a child could possibly be expected to honor parents coming from negative situations, other than to start with forgiveness. Forgiveness will yield freedom and healing. It's highly probable that parents who are suffering in their brokenness pass it on to their children, but breaking generational behavior patterns is an option open to all of us.

I've heard stories of people having terrible childhoods, and the redemption stories are miraculous! One notable story comes to mind from the lead singer of one of my favorite bands, Mercy Me. Bard Willard suffered such abuse, but through God's powerful ways, his heart healed and brought his father to know God. Before his father died, Bard was able to honor his father by caring for him in his final days. We can't begin to know what God can and will do even in the most unthinkable circumstances, but having faith, hope, and trust in stories like Bard's teaches us that when we are relentless to seek honoring God, even when is difficult to understand, we will be blessed.

Blessings come in all forms, and one such blessing is my beautiful blended family. More than ever before, the blended family is a common dynamic. I am a stepchild, I have a stepparent (Father Jim), and I'm a stepmother, so there's pretty much no combination in this dynamic I've not experienced. There are situations I've been told in which a child will claim, "This is my mother's husband or my father's wife, not my parent," with a resistance to honor or respect their stepparent. This may have nothing to do with the stepparent, but nonetheless it's a real emotion by a child struggling to honor a parent, "step" or not. So are they supposed to anyway? I don't know, other than we are called to love our neighbor and walk in the fruits of the Spirit, so my best guess is yes.

For me, it was an easy decision to love my stepfather well, but there was another stepfather before Jim who posed a more complicated dynamic. He was important to me as an adolescent and only for a season. Nonetheless, my desire was for positive relationships then and now.

The circumstances that lead to having a stepparent can be the result of a divorce or the passing of a parent, but for children, there's an abyss of unknown expectations ahead. What kind of relationship will be modeled for them? Regardless, being prompted to have a healthy marriage could be the outcome of a bad example. It's all so complicated and a reason why I believe God doesn't like divorce, but fortunately many blended families are positive redemption for children and their parents.

I'm not saying this with any arrogance, but I believe my stepson Paul and I have a wonderful relationship! I attribute his kindness toward me to who he is at the core and how he was raised with love. Knowing my place in our family has likely helped him love me as much as I love him. Imagining how Paul might feel with me coming into his world, from experience, helped me frame our relationship as the adult. As a result, I feel honor from him. Although he may not be obligated by this commandment, he walks it out, and from my perspective, I believe he is and will continue to be blessed by doing so. I know I am!

There are still questions I can't answer, however. Honoring our father and mother demands respect and restraint that may not always be warranted. If we want to honor God and receive

His blessings for honoring our parents, it doesn't seem fair that not all children are operating on the same curve. So as I have been contemplating all this, I default to prayer. I needed wisdom to find answers or at least peace in case I might not find them right away, and in prayer I knew I would find what I was searching for.

It's wise to pray for our specific needs. In this case, how to honor unhealthy parents or stepparents is the question, while wanting to please God and receive His blessings. If you struggle with what to say or how to pray, which I've experienced before, starting with a familiar scripture is a good beginning. Luke 11:1–4 says that one of Jesus's disciples asked Him,

> "Lord, teach us to pray, as John taught his disciples." And he said to them, "When you pray, say:
> "Father, hallowed be your name,
> Your kingdom come.
> Give us each day our daily bread.
> And forgive us our sins,
> for we ourselves forgive everyone who is
> indebted to us.
> And lead us not into temptation."

Praying the Lord's Prayer is the perfect place to begin when we are challenged with our questions and looking for wisdom. It's also the prayer that reminds us that God will provide for us and forgive us if we simply ask Him. If we speak with God as we want our children to speak with us, it becomes much more comfortable. The more we talk with God, we will realize He's approachable and wants to be a part of even the smallest decisions weighing on our shoulders.

If we've been fortunate, we've had a father and mother who are approachable, but it isn't always the case. What do those without these accepting nurturers at home have as an alternative? Where can these children go for answers? Practically it can be intimidating to confide in an adult if you've been hurt or let down by another adult, especially if it was a parent. Our Father God, however, is always there for us, is always approachable, will always comfort us, and is ready to provide answers for us.

God simply wants us to come to Him, trust Him, confide in Him, and repent to Him, just as I want my children to be comfortable talking and sharing their hearts, desires, hurts, and dreams with me. God is waiting for us to do the same with Him. Lean into the wisdom of prayer, no matter how great or small the conversation. It may seem silly to us, but nothing is too small for God to handle. Once we tap into this place of relationship with God, we surely will be wiser by hearing and learning more from our Father. Matthew 6:33 says, "Seek first the kingdom of God and his righteousness, and all these things will be added to you." That's where we often stop reading (or singing), but there's more. Matthew 6:34 goes on to say, "Therefore do not be anxious about tomorrow, for tomorrow will be anxious for itself. Sufficient for the day is its own trouble."

We should pray for today and trust that God has our backs for tomorrow. He takes care of today, so of course He will take care of tomorrow too. I have another dear friend who shared a moment in her childhood when she heard her heavenly Father speak to her His words and promise to take care of her. Her circumstances were very difficult, so I loved hearing this story from her. Too often we want proof that He is listening, so sharing our stories with others can encourage as well as offer wisdom that can be valuable in another's life.

There's also wisdom in prayer and in seeking God first versus our friends, work colleagues, the daily horoscope, family, and even our parents. That's not to say we aren't to ever talk with our trusted family or friends about challenges, but what I believe Jesus means and the Bible says is to go to God first. "Seek ye first the kingdom of God" is what scripture says, not "Wait till after you've talked with everyone else and still feel stressed out and confused and don't know what to do—then seek Me." It's the same with our earthly parents; often we look for solutions ourselves before seeking their counsel. It can be a good thing in certain situations for children to attempt solutions on their own, but if filled with pride, it may not be the best approach at all and possibly foolish.

That said, I've done this precise thing countless times; I've looked everywhere and to everyone for answers and discounted that praying will matter. As a matter of fact, it's actually funny that once I "got it" and started praying first, I grew amused at how silly I had been for so, *so* long, doing everything but seeking God first. I've had conversations with people who practically brush off the idea of praying as a real valid option for answers, as if that will actually solve the problem or produce a better outcome. The truth is, it will and it does. Wisdom in learning from our mistakes, learning from others, and seeking others' input is a good thing. Seeking God first, however, is necessary in my opinion for us to be in the relationship He desires from us as our Father and also to benefit from what He wants to reveal.

We want our children to talk with us, and God wants us to talk with Him, and not just when we need Him. We don't want our children to call us only when they need something from us or when there's exciting news to share. We want to hear about all parts of their lives and be included in all the little parts too, not just the highlights. We ought to consider this when evaluating our relationship with God and recognize He wants us to share all of ourselves with Him. First Thessalonians 5:16–18 says, "Rejoice always, pray without ceasing, give thanks in all circumstances; for this is the will of God in Christ Jesus for you."

God is our Father. We are to honor Him and His commandments, and He will bless us. He has entrusted us as parents to care for our children, and our children are asked to honor us, and they too will be blessed. It seems so obviously placed before us to understand, so it interests me how some children today, young and adult children, have resisted showing honor to their parents as God has asked.

When we ask our heavenly Father for specific things, He doesn't always give us what we want. Similarly, we don't always grant the requests of our children, but it can be hard to say no. It's likely He's protecting us when we hear "no," but regardless, we want to give our children the desires of their hearts, just as the Lord wants to give us the desires of our hearts.

When we don't get what we want from our Father, do we react with humility, or are we mad at God? Children can react with anger and frustration too, so do we allow these responses from our children or help our children navigate this terrain with respect and deserved honor? The push-pull of literally and figuratively fighting for independence and finding it out the hard way isn't new. There's a healthy amount of latitude we should allow children in figuring "it" out for themselves. Encouraging our children that they have the free will to make decisions for themselves while honoring us bears an interesting similarity to how God offers us free will to do the same.

When I think about honoring my own father and mother, I feel a combination of peace, joy, and sadness: peace because I have repented for the times I dishonored my parents; joy because I am humbled by my parents' grace and His grace, but a little sad too; sad because I'm seeing my opportunity to honor my mother slip away as she's aging, and sad as I wasn't able to amply honor my father, since he died when I was only eleven. I am able to still honor his memory, which I do, but I would love to glean just a little of his wisdom.

I can't help but think about the wise owl when thinking of my dad and wisdom. The last gift my dad gave me before he died was a stuffed animal owl I treasured, so I've always been fascinated by the fluffy creature. Not knowing why an owl symbolized wisdom, I found a few distinct yet unrelated theories as to how the owl became synonymous with wisdom. One is from ancient Greek mythology relating the owl as a favored pet to the goddess of wisdom, Athena. With several stories connecting Athena and the owl, somehow the symbolism stuck. A more natural interpretation is that owls have large, "smart"-looking eyes, keen night vision, and impeccable hearing, making them smart predators.

Wise or not, we don't seek wisdom from owls, but what about seeking wisdom from other sources? Mediums, fortunetellers, and horoscopes are all able to influence our thinking. We ought to be cautious in our explorations for answers and those in whom we invest our hope for wisdom. I believe God encourages us to seek wisdom, however, but from those He's granted wisdom to. He's imparted wisdom to people of influence all around us. Like my earthly father, who taught me what it felt like to be loved, my mother has always sprinkled wisdom into my life. My favorite piece of wisdom from her that I still refer to is "When in doubt, don't do it." This gem of wisdom has served me well many times over. She has imparted much more wisdom, including the treasure of a smile, the need to stand up straight, the value in a handwritten note, the importance of grace, and the absolute necessity of prayer.

My parents' wisdom was a responsibility they likely felt important to pass along to my brother and me. Much wisdom is passed down generation to generation, so it must be good, or we wouldn't keep sharing it. There's a simple truth to being older and wiser. Parents have a unique opportunity to share wisdom not only with their children but also with their children's friends and of course those willing and open to being mentored or advised. The moms in particular who helped raise me, as well as parents in my adult years who have influenced me, had many treasures of wisdom to impart—some original, but others more familiar:

- "Accept the invitation, even if you don't feel up to going." You may be the light of their day. People ask you because they enjoy your company, and you never know what joy you could bring to them.
- "It'll get better before you get married" Whether a skinned knee or a broken heart, you will heal. (Elsie Crank)
- "There's always a silver lining" Don't let the adversity consume you because there's always good in a bad situation. There's a lesson to be learned in the adversity. (Mildred Cooper)

- "Just open the Bible and read a little every day. Seek a relationship with Christ."
- "Quit trying to change people." We aren't the authors of changing others, that's up to God. We can however change ourselves and how we respond to others. (Donna Hearne)
- "Nothing good happens after midnight." Whatever you're doing after midnight is often coupled with trouble or consequences you would surely be wise to avoid.
- "One won't, two might, but three will." Beware of the company you keep and the temptations that come with being in a group. (Marilyn Pendergast)
- "Just break it down." You don't need to be overwhelmed by your situation or circumstances. Tackle one piece at a time, and all will work out. (my children's grandfather, Bigdaddy, H. Dawson French)
- "If you can't say anything nice, don't say anything at all." (my grandmother, Ginger Mitchell)

What wisdom are we sharing with others? Do we stay silent? Are we mentoring and discipling others? Do we stop sharing wisdom beyond our children or family members? How can we be sure what we are sharing is right? We need to ask God for wisdom but also ask God whom to share it with and when. I have a tendency to insert my two cents, believing I'm doing a good thing, but am I? The wisdom I believe I should share isn't always God-ordained or welcomed, so it's been an exercise of restraint in recent years to verify my intentions and my part in the situation and, most importantly, discern if the so-called wisdom I believe is in fact wisdom from the Lord rather than my own opinion.

When we pray for wisdom, what we are to do with the wisdom God has given us may still require additional wisdom. In our eagerness to take action, we can miss what comes next. There are times we may need to do nothing and wait for His cue to lead us. Hearing His wisdom or wisdom He's placed in those who love us and care about us is the pathway to answers we seek. "If any of you lacks wisdom, let him ask God, who gives generously to all without reproach, and it will be given him. But let him ask in faith, with no doubting, for the one who doubts is like a wave of the sea that is driven and tossed by the wind" (James 1:5–6).

Our Father is waiting for us to ask Him for wisdom, but He also given us the resources to find it. The Holy Spirit within us is His voice; His words in the Bible, including the Ten Commandments, are His wisdom granted to us as His children. "All Scripture is breathed out by God and profitable for teaching, for reproof, for correction, and for training in righteousness, that the man of God may be complete, equipped for every good work" (2 Timothy 3:16–17).

Knowing where to find wisdom is part of the formula to guide us; the rest of the formula comes in trusting what we find. Once we hear from our Father, do we question it, doubt it, or ignore it? I know I have done all of the above. God's wisdom is the shortcut for clarity, plain and simple. As the disciple James says, we should have faith in the wisdom God is giving us and not doubt it. If we are asking and truly want to know the answers we seek, why can't we just accept what is clear from the Lord? Just as with trusting our parents, we need to trust God and not make it harder than it needs to be.

Trust hasn't always been easy for me. Losing my father at such a young age, combined with receiving several confusing messages from supposed trustworthy men, contributed largely to my challenge with trust. I wasn't a wary person by nature or even cynical about relationships. I was typically hopeful and a romantic, possibly to a fault, but I realized, after many years of self-reflection and countless attempts to "unpack" books, counseling, and conversations with family and confidants, that at the core I didn't fully trust anyone to love me, provide for me, and not abandon me. In some ways this lack of trust motivated me, inspiring ambition, drive, and, ultimately, reliance on myself over anyone, including God!

Without realizing it, I found myself letting God off the hook because I didn't want to bug Him, waste His time with my needs, or arrogantly wait on Him to comfort me the way I thought I needed to be comforted. I was doing Him a favor but was so busy looking for solutions that I didn't notice they were already available to me. It's like that expression: you can't see the forest for the trees. We're so caught up in the minutiae of all that's around us that we can't see what are right in front of us—answers! "And after the earthquake a fire, but the Lord was not in the fire. And after the fire the sound of a low whisper" (1 Kings 19:12). In silence we are able to hear God's whisper, so seeking occasions to relish in silence allowed me to start noticing God's affirming love. Simply put, there's wisdom in listening to God, which takes us back to the importance of prayer, honoring the Sabbath, and dedicating time to seek Him, so we can be tuned in to hearing what He is saying to us.

Stay cautious not to rush through daily devotional time or hurry through a quick prayer to check a box, not to half-listen to a sermon or skim through a Bible verse. We may miss His words that we really needed to hear or read that day: wisdom. My mom has wisely reiterated, "Haste makes waste," many times. Could we possibly be wasting an opportunity to hear God's answers to our prayers? Asking God for wisdom is asking God to be the leader of our lives, so we must allow Him to be the leader and be careful not to get in the way. We will know peace; we will be in a stronger relationship with our Father, the way parents want to be in strong relationship with their children. And as children, isn't this what we want, to be in an amazing relationship with our parents and our Lord?

God commands us to honor our earthly father and mother, and He exhorts us to abide by His commandments. If we do both, the blessings are abundant. From my firsthand experience, God has strengthened my marriage, healed relationships, protected me beyond measure, provided for me in abundance, granted me good health, and restored my soul over and over again. These are only a few of the many blessings I've received, and although there has been sadness, suffering, and frustrations at times and in seasons, I've always felt loved and aware that I am His and that He has me in His righteous right hand, no matter what! "Fear not, for I am with you; be not dismayed, for I am your God; I will strengthen you, I will help you, I will uphold you with my righteous right hand" (Isaiah 41:10).

As a mother bird protects her babies, this mama bird protects hers too. My children will all tell you there's no counting the times I've said my love cup is filled when all my chicks are in the nest, and they also can tell you that I have and will defend them and fight for them with all that I have. So will God continue to fight for all of us!

Now, as I'm watching Mom suffer from her disease, I want to honor her with as much patience and dignity as possible. When my father died, I was too young to understand the toll this took on my mom. She was brave beyond my comprehension, and later she shared with me the blessing she felt having both my brother Randy and me. Having us to care for provided her purpose, comfort, and healing in her grief. She felt so blessed to have us, she said, and even though we didn't realize it, we helped her heal. As a matter of fact, my mom took Randy and me on a six-week trip the summer after we lost my dad. The three of us journeyed from Little Rock through Texas, Colorado, Wyoming, Seattle, Montana, South Dakota, and finally up to our beloved northern Michigan. We had amazing adventures from rafting the Snake River to seeing Old Faithful, from visiting family in Seattle to roadside picnics; we did it together!

Looking back, I'm amazed at my mom's strength and grateful we had each other in that difficult time. To honor her now is my blessing. In these precious moments I have today, honoring her and caring for her as she cared for me, it's full circle blessings and all the more reason we are to be obedient to God's commandments; we don't want to miss out on any of His blessings! "Blessed are those whose way is blameless, who walk in the law of the Lord! Blessed are those who keep his testimonies, who seek him with their whole heart, who also do no wrong, but walk in his ways!" (Psalm 119:1–3)

WHAT ARE YOUR THOUGHTS?

1) On a scale of 1 to 10, how would you rate yourself in honoring your father and mother? Is there a specific time you remember not honoring them?

_____

_____

_____

_____

2) Do you believe it's more challenging for children to honor their parents today with the added outside available influences?

_____

_____

_____

_____

3) Are you comfortable sharing your "real" wisdom with others, particularly when it's unsolicited?

_____

_____

_____

_____

4) When you pray for specific wisdom regarding decisions in your life, how has it impacted the outcome?

_____

_____

_____

_____

SEVEN

WHAT WE WORSHIP

Gluttony, Lust, Greed, Anger, Sloth, Envy, Pride

> If then you have been raised with Christ, seek the
> things that are above, where Christ is, seated at
> the right hand of God. Set your minds on things
> that are above, not on things that are on earth.
>
> —Colossians 3:1–2

The Bible tells us that God is a jealous God. Serving or worshipping other "gods" makes Him jealous. "You shall not bow down to them or serve them, for I the Lord your God am a jealous God" (Exodus 20:5). What constitutes another god? is then the question. Physical idols of any sort, including objects, another person, and ourselves or anything that distracts us from God first is what I believe to be the answer. There are many things that count as such distractions, many of which are among the seven deadly sins. For as long as I can remember, I've known about the seven deadly sins but haven't paid much attention until recently to whether in fact they are sins. If they are sins and God is the author, why didn't He make seventeen initial commandments to Moses instead of the original ten? And why are there specifically seven? Why not eight or another ten as an addendum to the original ten?

Throughout the Bible, the number seven is mentioned over seven hundred times, so maybe this is no coincidence. To some, seven represents God's perfection and is a symbol of spiritual completeness. God chose this number with intent—seven days in the week and seven colors in the rainbow, for example—and there are several more phenomena with seven, from seven continents to seven musical notes to the seven seals and seven trumpets in the book of Revelation. This fascinates me!

One of my favorite spirit filled authors, Dutch Sheets, wrote about the number seven in one of his daily messages in GiveHim15.com. He said,

> The number seven is associated with covenants and marriage. In ancient times, when two people entered into a covenant, they swore an oath, repeating it seven times. This is most likely because the number seven symbolizes "completion," and the individuals were "completely" giving themselves to the other in covenant. This oath was actually called "sevening oneself." In fact, the word "seven" and "oath" come from the same Hebrew word! Seven, therefore, symbolizes covenant and marriage.

After reading these thoughts from Dutch, and acknowledging seven has many unique placements in not only the Bible but our world, I believe God uses the number seven intentionally. If seven is God's number to signify a covenant and completeness, it makes sense that we would strive to be in complete covenant with God. In other words, it's hard to be in covenant with God if we're living out any sins or sinful behaviors on a daily basis, even the deadly ones—deadly because if we don't die to our sins, we can't live fully in Christ. "We know that Christ, being raised from the dead, will never die again; death no longer has dominion over him. For the death he died he died to sin, once for all, but the life he lives he lives to God. So you also must consider yourselves dead to sin and alive to God in Christ Jesus" (Romans 6:9–11).

All of this sounds divinely scripted, up to the point where there's no one place God wrote the seven deadly sins in the Bible. If He didn't write them, who then was the author, when and why were they created, and does God's number seven have an application here, or is it mere happenstance that there are seven? Much research supports early innovators of theology as originators of this list of seven underlying causes that lead to sin. One such discovery comes from the Catholic Church in the first century, from Tertullian of Carthage. He was the first to itemize these seven deadly conducts, but why seven remains a mystery, other than it's believed possibly because the number does represent wholeness.

After Christianity was legalized in AD 313, a Christian monk named Evagrius Ponticus wrote letters of concern to his fellow monks of what was known as the "eight evil thoughts," which were gluttony, lust, greed, anger, sloth, sadness, vanity, and pride. Ponticus, in the Eastern Christian church, was concerned that these particular eight thoughts could "interfere with their spiritual practice." Over the course of many centuries, these thoughts morphed from Greek to Latin and were ultimately refined by Thomas Aquinas in the thirteenth century into what we know today as the seven deadly sins.

Judging our disposition when distracted by these behaviors and not fully loving God, we can draw the conclusion that sin is sin, Walker says. In effect, these behaviors exhibit a need to fill a void in our lives where God should be first. Although Walker is not unique in his age group, it is unusual for these behaviors to be recognized as sin. What we're missing and how we're filling the void may not look like sins listed in the Ten Commandments, but if we acknowledge these behaviors as sin, it could be that we do not truly love God as He asks. We may be worshipping other gods, false idols.

I've said many times to my children that if we don't deal with what's hurting in our hearts today, at some point emotions will manifest, and typically not in a healthy way. This can look like multitudes of challenges from addictions to distorted view of success, which can ultimately cost us everything. Fulfillment in and from God will fill these voids. How do we come to know true joy? Dying to our sins, including the deadly ones, and focusing on Christ to complete us! The gift of Christ dying on the cross for us gives us hope of this promise. The alternative is to love ourselves more than we love God, which can have optics of sabotage and idolatry of self. False idols are not to be worshipped; only God is to be worshipped! If we know these truths, I'm challenged to understand why we continue to engage in destructive behaviors that stunt our spiritual growth.

We have a concrete list of Commandments we need not break. Are we complicating obedience to God by adding these seven too? I believe the seven deadly sins are gateways subtly hindering our relationship with God that lead to breaking one of the ten. Pride, gluttony, and sloth are the deadly sins I struggle with the most. Lust, envy, greed, and anger have crept into my life, no doubt, but they aren't what continue to challenge me the way pride, gluttony, and sloth do. There are threads and patterns connecting these seven deadly sins to how joyful and peaceful our life can feel. For me, although I feel joyful and at peace much of the time, I'm aware that I'm still battling these sinful behaviors. I think about not only resting in joy and peace, but also my purpose from God. If I'm busy being prideful or full of sloth, can I be accomplishing God's call in my life? Have I wasted opportunities to do God's will?

These are questions I ask myself. If I'm feeling lazy, is it actually laziness or do I have a good excuse? Have I been staying present in prayer and discernment? I've spent countless minutes wondering if lying still, being quiet, resting on a "work" day, or skipping chores to simply "be still" has been in vain or part of a discipline to hear God speak to me. Possibly there's been healing happening from various life challenges and times of reflection sprinkled into these moments, but admittedly, there have also been simply lazy days and avoidance of facing the day. Is this considered sloth?

Having quiet still times in our lives in order to hear the Lord is vital. We need to be cautious that we aren't confusing those times meant for prayer and listening to God with doing nothing to grow in our spiritual life. According to the *Merriam Webster Dictionary*, *sloth* means disinclination to action or labor; inclination to laziness and spiritual apathy and inactivity. Proverbs 19:15–16 says, "Slothfulness casts into a deep sleep, and an idle person will suffer hunger. Whoever keeps the commandment keeps his life; he who despises his ways will die."

There are definitely seasons of my life when I've been less active in my faith journey. I can recall several times when the enemy was taunting me with guilt when I was feeling led to be still. We so often feel as though we have to be doing something— anything other than nothing at all. Simply put, when is it okay to do nothing, and how do we know it's okay and not the devil plotting for us to be slothful?

It's almost as if there's a deadly sin missing: busyness. We're conditioned to always be doing, going, working, playing, running, fixing, or planning, which *looks* like the opposite of sloth. But if we are in our busyness and aren't growing in our spiritual life and using our spiritual gifts, we may not recognize sloth as disrupting our relationship with God. There've been times when I've stayed busy serving for the church, all the while not paying attention to my spiritual growth or lack thereof. Quite honestly I have been wrapped up in doing "works" for God's approval much more than using some of those times to listen to the Holy Spirit for my growth. Participating and serving in the church is of paramount importance but it can't be in lieu of spiritual maturation. They go hand in hand, and this is where I've experienced personal slothfulness.

Practical ways to move the needle away from sloth and toward growth in our spiritual lives are plenty. For me, listening to worship music, spending time in silence with the Lord, time in prayer, participating in daily devotionals, reading books, and engaging with other faith-filled people inspire and feed me. All of these actions coupled with accountability to my incredible church small group are measures that sloth can't penetrate. Our spiritual health and activity are necessary for our relationship with God to develop into something stronger. Being in a deep sleep, apathetic, or slothful stunts us, and we are called to be good stewards of the life we've been given. Our challenge is to recognize the difference between sloth and necessary stillness. "You keep him in perfect peace whose mind is stayed on you, because he trusts in you" (Isaiah 26:3).

Avoiding sloth isn't my only sinful struggle; another is gluttony! Possibly a harder discipline to harness is my favorite gluttonous food indulgences, which vacillate between chips and homemade sweets. Chips typically trump chocolate and all my other guilty pleasures. If you looked in my pantry, you would find all the healthy treats, but peppered in between are my secret stashes of goodies that Curt dares not invade. What's wrong with indulging ourselves in delicious foods or a variety of guilty pleasures? I'm not sure there's anything wrong on occasion, but the question to ask is, are we also indulging in the Lord?

To indulge means to satisfy a desire and enjoy the pleasure

of something in particular. I've wondered recently if I crave time with God as much as grabbing my favorite snacks or overindulging on streaming a popular TV series or scrolling social media. Is this even a big deal? I don't believe it's sin to eat chips, watch TV, or check my social presence, but if I overeat, binge-watch, or consume a gross serving of the world's influences, it can become gluttonous and create distance between God and us.

The same applies to anything in excess. Where are our thoughts and attentions when we wake up each morning? Observing what comes to mind, my to-do list or saying good morning to Jesus, jump-started my awareness to this very question. If we are reaching for the phone when we first wake up in search of the world's top stories before talking with Jesus, we may need a reset. Wondering what's happening in the world before our feet hit the floor can become a gluttonous habit—and not a healthy one, I might add.

Awakening our hearts and minds to hear the Lord as we open our eyes each morning is the truth we ought to seek. What a wonderful time to take in His presence, His love, warmth, wisdom, and words. Many of us try to adhere to this routine and some do it with ease, but in essence, the point is as a culture it seems that we're tempted to worship the world more than God and we often do it unknowingly. "You shall have no other gods before me" (Exodus 20:3).

Why do we care so much what the world has to say? When I desire something else to fill me more than the Lord, I believe it stems from a lack of faith in God for fulfillment, a lack of self-control, or a dependence on something else for temporary satisfaction. Our journey to know ourselves will surely reveal the root of gluttonous behavior. Although I have my opinions, it's not up to me to diagnose the "why" in someone else, but observing my neighbor's nature does offer insight to ask myself "why?"

Gluttony is defined as excess eating or drinking, according to

Merriam Webster. It also means greedy or excessive indulgence. "Do you not know that you are God's temple and that God's Spirit dwells in you? If anyone destroys God's temple, God will destroy him. For God's temple is holy, and you are that temple" (1 Corinthians 3:16–17). Gluttony isn't just stuffing our faces or pigging out on yummy snacks and home-baked goodies. It's also prevalent in habits with alcohol, shopping, watching TV, playing golf, or frankly anything that we consume in excess.

None of this translates to honoring our bodies according to scripture. It's actually the opposite, so why do we do it? What prompts gluttony: sadness, boredom, avoidance, and loneliness? The expression *emotional eater* comes to mind. Looking for comfort in food is all too common, but on the flip side, what's my excuse when I'm feeling joyful? So often we celebrate with food and occasionally splurge. I don't believe this is necessarily gluttony, and I'm all for feasting from time to time, especially on vacation!

What other gluttonous tendencies do we commonly overlook? The cliché *gluttons for punishment* evolved from repeating our sinful behaviors with no real gain for the kingdom. We've all most likely said this one time or another, so we know what we're doing is in excess and possibly risky and will come with a consequence. But we're all right with that consequence and indulge anyway— at least until we're forced or make a choice to stop. Ironically, fasting is a good way to practice awareness of what is filling us and acknowledging what we really are hungry or thirsty for is something else, God!

I used to be so obsessed with my Diet Coke and unsweet iced tea addictions that I almost ruined a vacation and friendship over having to get my fix. Don't believe me? Just ask my best friend Mary Neal, and she will confirm this silly truth. We were in California for a few days on a girls' trip. All was well until there was a threat to not find my unsweet iced tea. I was slapped in the face by the reality that I was irrational over a beverage.

A drink had control over me. I went from iced tea to Diet Coke and back; I had to have one (or two) every day or I wasn't myself— or so I thought. I had become obsessed every day with having to having it. I would go out of my way just to satisfy my dependence. The behavior became my dependence to set my day straight versus making sure my day was going well because I had consumed my Jesus. Now, if and when I indulge, it's a choice I weigh. I've got full knowledge of my decision and why I allow myself to dive in … this once.

> I say, walk by the Spirit, and you will not gratify the desires of the flesh. For the desires of the flesh are against the Spirit, and the desires of the Spirit are against the flesh, for these are opposed to each other, to keep you from doing the things you want to do. But if you are led by the Spirit, you are not under the law. Now the works of the flesh are evident: sexual immorality, impurity, sensuality, idolatry, sorcery, enmity, strife, jealousy, fits of anger, rivalries, dissensions, divisions, envy, drunkenness, orgies, and things like these. I warn you, as I warned you before, that those who do such things will not inherit the kingdom of God. (Galatians 5:16–21)

This scripture seems very clear and upsetting at the same time! Does this mean that if I've ever acted in a fit of anger, had too much to drink, or been jealous, I'm not going to inherit the kingdom of God? Insert the fear of God here for me, because I definitely want to go to heaven, and I know I've succumbed to the works of the flesh, according to Paul in Galatians. It can be confusing to non-theologians and less advanced biblical students like me to reconcile it all. I have to remind myself that the ultimate answers to my questions all boil down to obedience, repentance, and the knowledge that I've asked Christ to be my Savior, and my salvation isn't a dangling carrot from the Lord. He knew we would all fall short, so He sent His son to die on the cross for our sins, including the deadly ones.

It's important to have awareness of our struggles and how they are connected to our relationship with God and His commandments. If we aren't worshipping these false idols, we are less likely to fall into the traps of behaviors like anger for instance. The opposite of anger is patience, kindness, and understanding. "A fool gives full vent to his spirit, but a wise man quietly holds it back" (Proverbs 29:11). "Be not quick in your spirit to become angry, for anger lodges in the heart of fools" (Ecclesiastes 7:9).

These two scriptures warn us against anger, and our default response to a bevy of frustrations is often anger. Once I step back and allow my emotions to settle down, prudence typically prevails, and I don't act on my knee-jerk emotion. This has taken time, practice, prayer, and maturity. I've found that by approaching situations with a level head instead of a flustered rage, I not only avoid wasting precious energy making a fool of myself, I also feel a certain peace. Does this mean I get it right every time? No! Curt and my children can attest that the irrational Libby still appears once in a blue moon. I hope they can also tell you I'm a calmer version of myself as a result of depending on God for my understanding instead of my own. "Trust in the Lord with all your heart, and do not lean on your own understanding" (Proverbs 3:5).

What are we so irritated about anyway? Some people are "just plain-ole' mean." They may be hurt people, hurting people. Do angry people just try to make someone else mad for sport? Have you noticed that when we kill someone with kindness if they're angry, it makes us feel better and can end up defusing their anger? It can cause them to pause on why and how they're acting. We may not be able to control another person's anger, but we can control our own. If we do our part, we may be setting an example for others to see. Watching other people "go there" is unattractive; showing unrighteous anger looks wasteful, unnecessary, and petty. So why do we tend to react this way sometimes? What is at the root of our unrestricted reactions? "Be angry and do not sin; do not let the sun go down on your anger, and give no opportunity to the devil" (Ephesians 4:26–27).

I love this scripture. God is telling us exactly what to do; yet we may default to allowing ourselves to make it worse. We all process differently, so in fairness, what's easy for some to get over takes others longer to digest. My nature is to address the issues head-on when possible and not go to bed angry. This is what I believe is best. Some would argue that oldie, "Time heals all wounds." I agree it does, but in the meantime, let's be reminded not to permit pride to overrule compassion and healing.

Anger can get the best of all of us. Righteous anger in particular seems heightened when we see blatant wrongs or an egregious offense toward the innocent. I'm talking about the hairs-rising-on-your-neck anger: an adult treating your child unfairly or any child being abused provokes righteous anger. There are injustices that make us angry; that is justified in my mind. God showed righteous anger many times in the Bible, sometimes against evil and sometimes toward His most faithful. Although He was angered, most often it was met with grace and mercy. In 2 Samuel, God was angry with David but showed him mercy. If God can get angry with His beloved children, of course we will experience righteous anger too. Even though we love the Lord, we will fail, but God knew we would sin; that's why He sent a Savior, to rescue us from ourselves. Asking God to convict our hearts and minds for redirection toward Him versus the anger we default to is one step toward positive change.

If we have doubt that the seven deadly sins are sin, Dawson argues that not only are they sin, but blindingly so. He says they distract us from being rational and take us down paths of bad decisions, not paths to follow God. They are all devil-related behaviors steeped in nonspiritual perspectives. We have our eyes off the ball of the Lord's will, and our hearts are distracted by bad intentions rather than pure and good intentions. Tim adds that if we pick any one of the seven deadly sins and find what's festering underneath, there lie the masters of our hearts. These are the false idols we worship. First John 2:16 says, "All that is in the world—the desires of the flesh and the desires of the eyes and the pride of life—is not from the Father but is from the world."

Is lust strictly physical though? The obvious definition of lust seems blatantly all about the physical craving of the flesh. It's not limited to the flesh, however; we may lust for a car, a home, jewelry, etc., but it's still seemingly physical. If not just physical though, consider how lust, greed, and envy are similar. Lust: we desire what we don't have for our pleasure. Greed: we want more of what we have for our pleasure. Envy: we want something we don't have for our pleasure. Pleasure in this case transfers feelings of temporary happiness, satisfaction, and enjoyment—*temporary* being the operative word.

Pleasure isn't necessarily a bad thing to desire. God designed us for His pleasure and for us to take pleasure in His creation. There is wondrous pleasure in walking by brooks, hiking in the woods, listening to the waves and symphonies from songbirds, or taking in any of His nature. He also created us to enjoy fellowship with His children and to be in delight. Our greatest pleasures, however, should be in God Himself, not anything of the world.

This is where we can find ourselves in a precarious place, looking for our hope, identity, or worth in false idols to save us. Ridding ourselves of these toxic behaviors will result in our ultimate pleasure. "If you abide in me, and my words abide in you, ask whatever you wish, and it will be done for you" (John 15:7).

I can see the temptations of lust and greed tangibly unfold all around me. It's not difficult to encounter; with the flip of a switch, we're flooded with what at least looks like greed. We can't ever know the true nature of our neighbor's heart, and it's not our concern, but we can check our own hearts. What are we holding on to? Are we generous or greedy with our time, resources, and intentions? Greed isn't always obvious and it can be particular to circumstances. I sometimes struggle not to be greedy with my time. I love spending time with my family, with my people, and for my purpose, but beyond that, I tend to need a pep talk with myself to give it away—unless it's my idea. Then I'm extremely generous with my time. So a little greedy possibly, yet I will give and give of my resources otherwise. I think we tend to tie greed to money, but money doesn't have a monopoly when it comes to greed. In any form greed is of and for self. That said, there's a rich opportunity to shift greedy desires toward generosity.

Envy has me a little more perplexed than greed and lust in terms of seeking for pleasure. I get what envy means—to have a painful or resentful desire for another's advantages—but in my heart I feel blessed and very full. Yet sometimes I still feel envy. There are people who are envious and bitter toward those who seemingly have what they want. This is an offense to God in my opinion, as if to say He is being questioned about how He blesses us. I don't succumb to this envy, although I may have at one time.

My "now envy" is envying my friends who have their parents and children living in the same town. Most of my family lives in four different states, so to see them in person means a lot of traveling. It means not always being together for special occasions and missing out on more frequent hugs. The flip side of this particular envy is that my time spent with loved ones is always intentional and never taken for granted. I've attempted to shift my envy to gratitude, which helps a lot. That said, I am still a little envious!

I also envy marriages that have withstood the difficulties and challenges sure to attack even the strongest marriage. Curt and I have talked many times about the consequences of divorce from our prior marriages. We won't ever know how God would have grown us and reconciled us in those marriages, but we are wiser in our marriage as a result of the experiences. God is now at the head of our marriage. He has also used us to disciple others in their marriages. Turning my envy of lasting marriages into now having a marriage others could admire is an example of God's presence and redemption. For couples who have overcome obstacles and remained married through them all, we respect you but still envy you a little.

The Lord has showered us with His abundance and grace and is more generous to us than we deserve. I believe He wants us to fulfill His purpose for us, and envy, greed, or any selfishness can hijack that purpose. If we have our own agenda from lustful desires and beyond, we are pursuing what's fleeting rather than pursuing God and our purpose. We tend to pursue what we think will save us, which is typically more money, a certain lifestyle or status, more stuff, and oftentimes a person. If we chase a person to fill us, we're not depending on God to fill us. We believe we need more than what is already enough. It's an exhausting amount of energy to strategize to get what we want. We see this happening in our world all around us, people acting entitled to take more than what is theirs, and this spills into greed for power as well.

Why are we willing to risk long-term joy from our Father

for short-term or floundering fulfillment? Trying to get more of something else to feel good or to fill us versus relying on God to feel successful or whole could be warping our purpose from God. If we are focused on getting more than what we're given, we forget that what we have is purposeful and ample. If we worship ourselves, what we have, or those we can influence for our gain, then this becomes a clear commitment of disobedience to God. False idols and worshipping our gods can lead to catastrophic consequences, primarily our relationship with God, but also other relationships that may be more difficult to repair. "If we live by the Spirit, let us also keep in step with the Spirit. Let us not become conceited, provoking one another, envying one another" (Galatians 5:25–26). This may be easier said than done.

To live by the fruits of the Spirit, however, is a challenge I'm up to: love, joy, peace, patience, kindness, goodness, faithfulness, gentleness, and self-control. Curt and I were challenged to practice this mindset last year, and let me tell you that it isn't always easy. We have the fruits of the Spirit listed on pieces of paper around our house, with a framed version on the kitchen windowsill (thank you, Gregg and Lisa Greven). The kitchen is where we admittedly need reminding most! I don't know about you, but the kitchen is not only the heart of our home but also the epicenter of our most embarrassing verbal duels. Fortunately, one of us typically has the presence of mind to recall the fruits of the Spirit before long, and we find our way back toward a loving tone and productive conversation and away from sinful behavior.

Whether it is lust, envy, greed, or one of the other four deadly sins, when we allow our desires to trump God's desires for us, we are missing out on ultimate freedom. Freedom is on the other side of killing what's killing us, said someone once. The Holy Spirit lives within us to convict us toward a right relationship with Him. We want to be in agreement with God in order to recognize the gifts we have to serve Him and the church. We must rely on Him for His provisions. We don't have to lust for more, envy, or take more, because *what we have is divinely enough to complete us.* I've wondered: if we know that we are enough and what we have is enough, why do we still struggle with sinful behaviors? Who do we need to impress? Where is the transparency? Is it pride? Ah, the superstar sin nature! Some say it is the sin from which all others arise. "By insolence comes nothing but strife, but with those who take advice is wisdom" (Proverbs 13:10).

Advice is something I will ask for but not always follow, at least not without a serious cross-check and second opinion. It was amusing when I had my handwriting analyzed at the Arkansas state fair circa 1980, and my results said, "Often seeks advice but seldom takes it." Wow. I laughed at first and then wondered if it wasn't more of an insult than a compliment. We seek advice to get guidance or affirmation from others. Not taking it could be wisdom, but prideful hindrances may also be the reason. Believing that we know best and have all the answers and that we're smarter could be our pride speaking, but I also have felt a lack of trust to yield to another's approach because I trusted myself more.

My two cents is that pride stems from insecurity or possibly fear, or somewhere in the middle, and is our attempt to protect ourselves. "Protection from what?" is a question only we can answer. Maybe we've experienced hurt feelings. We can act as if we don't care or react in a haughty way, basically sin begetting more sin. Getting it out in the open and talking about our feeling with the fruits of the Spirit in mind would be beneficial. Instead, we may opt for struggling to admit being wrong and become defensive. Boy, have I experienced this pride. I wonder if it's because we're masking old wounds. Maybe it's our nature to don pride chainmail versus the armor of God. "Put on the whole armor of God, that you may be able to stand against the schemes of the devil" (Ephesians 6:11). If we protect ourselves with God's armor of truth, righteousness, and faith, this is all the protection we need, in my opinion. He beautifully designed us with all we need for safety, so we can ditch the pride!

He also created us in His image, so to Him we are all beautiful. I'm intrigued how we can get caught up in the pride of our outward appearance. From firm muscles to smooth skin and perfectly applied makeup to the latest clothing trends, putting our best selves on display isn't unique. Why we do it is what I call into question. If the pendulum swings from not caring at all to pride-filled excess about what is on the outside, we may need to redirect our focus to a contented happy medium. This coming from me, as I inspect my every outward imperfection and take inventory of what I can do to age a little more gracefully. Pride is a tough bullet to dodge, but an important one to take seriously.

Curt and I were on vacation in Florida not long ago and found ourselves in St. Augustine at the Ponce de Leon Fountain of Youth Archeological Park. The park was a combination of history and theater, which included dozens of peacocks roaming freely throughout the park. They were simply magnificent. I marveled at the intricately woven colors on display and wondered what God was thinking when He decorated each detail of these majestic creatures for our enjoyment. To say "proud as a peacock" almost seems justified when you consider they just might have a right to be proud. Take one look at these vibrant birds, and it makes perfect sense. Is there something wrong with this type of pride? There are people who are truly stunningly beautiful or are fit and trim; is this justified pride? If you're a peacock, I might say yes! Showing off those brilliant feathers to attract a mate likely works every time, but for you and me, the intent of what we're showing off can come across as desperate, arrogant, or prideful.

I believe there are moments of pride that are all right, given the intent of our hearts and if in purest form. Taking pride in our children's achievements or their character and taking a healthy pride in our achievements like building a house or creating lovely spaces are fitting expressions of pride. If I feel fortunate and know where my blessings come from, sharing with pride feels right. In other words, I'm proud to be one of God's children. "Far be it from me to boast except in the cross of our Lord Jesus Christ, by which the world has been crucified to me, and I to the world" (Galatians 6:14). Everything I have and all that I am is because of Jesus and what He did for me. To give God the glory brings me pride. It's not promoting us this time; it's promoting the kingdom.

We glorify Him by being obedient to His will and His commands and by improving our relationship with Him. Whether or not the seven deadly sins are sin is no longer a question for me. Anything that separates our hearts from nurturing and focusing on growing spiritually translates as sin in my opinion; we become what we chase. So the next time I notice the enemy lurking to my left, I pray the Holy Spirit provokes me to walk faster toward my Father's righteous arms to worship Him first. Recognizing that the enemy is attempting to distract me from living fully in relationship with God motivates me to toss my false idols to the curb. I aim to stop looking for loopholes or justifications of my behaviors and focus instead on how I can glorify God, atone for my sinful behaviors, and kick the habit(s) once and for all! "No temptation has overtaken you that is not common to man. God is faithful, and he will not let you be tempted beyond your ability, but with the temptation he will also provide the way of escape, that you may be able to endure it" (*1 Corinthians 10:13*).

WHAT ARE YOUR THOUGHTS?

> If you return to the Lord, your brothers and your
> children will find compassion with their captors
> and return to this land. For the Lord your God is
> gracious and merciful and will not turn away his
> face from you, if you return to him.
>
> —2 Chronicles 30:9

1) Do you believe the seven deadly sins are in fact sins? Why or
   why not?

_____

_____

_____

_____

2) Which of the seven deadly sins do you struggle with the most,
   and how can you actively attempt change?

_____

_____

_____

_____

3) If you were able to add another deadly sin, what would it be, and why?

_____

_____

_____

_____

4) Identify your false idols and what triggers you worshipping them.

_____

_____

_____

_____

EIGHT

LOVE

This is my commandment, that you love one another as I have loved you.

—John 15:12

My favorite word is *love*. Love portrays the intentions of my heart and wraps around me like a warm blanket. When I think about what drives me, brings me joy, and fills me up, it's love. I believe this is how God feels about us; He loves us and shows us His love in many ways every day. God = Love! Scripture tells us so!

We love because He first loved us. (1 John 4:19)

As the Father has loved me, so have I loved you. Abide in my love. (John 15:9)

Let all that you do be done in love. (1 Corinthians 16:14)

So now faith, hope, and love abide, these three; but the greatest of these is love. (1 Corinthians 13:13)

Therefore be imitators of God, as beloved children. And walk in love, as Christ loved us and gave himself up for us, a fragrant offering and sacrifice to God. (Ephesians 5:1–2)

If I dedicated this entire chapter, or for that matter this entire book, to these scriptures alone, it would capture the essence of all we need to know. God loves us, and He is asking us to love Him and love one another. It is written in Matthew 22:37–40,

And he said to him, "You shall love the Lord your God with all your heart and with all your soul and with all your mind. This is the great and first commandment. And a second is like it: You shall love your neighbor as yourself. On these two commandments depend all the Law and the Prophets."

Pastor Nick further explained to me what Jesus is teaching when Jesus tells His disciples of the greatest commandments; "He's basically underscoring what Moses told God's people" in Deuteronomy 6:5: "You shall love the Lord your God with all your heart and with all soul and with all your might." They're the framework for the direction of our hearts or like a mission statement for our relationship with God and others. The Commandments ask God's people to acknowledge Him as the one and only God. And they ask us, among other things, not to steal from our neighbor, murder our neighbor, or speak falsely or hurtfully of our neighbor. Jesus highlights what God is asking of us: to love Him and love our neighbor.

How do we learn to love as God is asking? To love literally means to have a feeling of strong or constant affection for a person, according to *Merriam Webster*. We are to love God first above all others, but are we feeling strong and constant affection for Him? If you've been in a relationship for any length of time, there are apt to be seasons of frustration. This can morph into the opposite of affection, so I believe we need to understand the biblical meaning of love in order to reference it when we may not be feeling it. We use the word *love* loosely at times, so to truly mean what we are saying, let's review what God says about love. "Love is patient and kind; love does not envy or boast; it is not arrogant or rude. It does not insist on its own way; it is not irritable or resentful; it does not rejoice at wrongdoing, but rejoices with the truth. Love bears all things, believes all things, hopes all things, endures all things" (1 Corinthians 13:4–7).

As we take steps closer to Christ through His Word with obedience, we develop compassion for others. This compassion evolves from apathy or discontentment and even pride or fear and will catapult us into sustainably loving others. Admittedly, there have been days I haven't felt love, not specifically from God but from someone else. So this raises the question, do we trust what we're feeling or draw from knowing what is truth? Feelings can be tricky, mostly because they're oftentimes not a reflection of reality.

Recently I wasn't feeling as though Curt and I were in sync because I wasn't feeling his typical attention. After a couple of brief conversations, I wised up to the reality that this was my imagination. Several piles on his plate distracted Curt, and simultaneously I had been distracted with my own piles. Perspective and rational thinking prevailed over my feelings, which weren't based in reality. All this to say that feelings can be real, but they can also be the enemy planting lies in our minds. When we remind ourselves of truth, the meaning of love, it's a fast track back to affection that is constant, which is love.

So often the simplest and clearest requests get muddled. What we're being taught by God is actually quite simple. I don't know about you, but I have struggled to follow God's simple ask. What I mean is that I intellectually know what He is asking of me. I've repeated the liturgical words lauding Him during worship for decades. On occasion, I've robotically said what I was conditioned to say in church at the prompted time during the service. I've prayed a prayer I always prayed without thinking about what I was praying. Words rolling off my tongue out of habit without reverence in what I was saying became more common than rare. Was I listening to what I was saying? Did I mean it? Believe it? Yes, I believed what I was saying, but I caught myself realizing I had been participating in a service yet not fully present in the experience of devotion to God. How could I know our Father if I wasn't paying attention to what He was saying? I always want Him to listen to me, and like any healthy relationship, this one is a two-way street, so I need to listen to Him … with intent!

My soul is convicted now more than ever to be present when I'm in worship, spiritual conversation, devotional time, and prayer time. It's important that I'm clear on what I'm praying and hearing from the Lord. When speaking about my faith, I need to use words that deliver my love for the Lord and what He's teaching me and asking of me. Giving God our undivided attention seems obvious, but we're human, and we may not always succeed in our efforts. The world is sometimes skewing our heart's intentions. Being in loving relationship of any kind, and in particular with God, demands that our hearts are willing and open to receive and express love. Speaking for myself, I strive to always show love toward God and my neighbor, but it doesn't always happen as I plan. I blame it all on sin, the master distracter.

If all we need is love to help us keep His commandments, they shouldn't be so difficult to follow; yet they can be. Why is this? We have the instructions and the recipe to be joyful and know true love. Most of us are eager to share our love and receive love. We're either pouring it out or trying to find it or feel it again. This is a common thread that connects us all, yet we tend to complicate it or overthink it. Love is a precious gift we seek to receive and give, yet often it's the most challenging part of our lives, whether in our relationship with a parent, child, spouse, family, or friends. Many familiar expressions about love say it best: "Love hurts," "Love is all you need," "Love makes the world go around," "Love conquers all." There's so much to say about the four-letter word. We talk, sing, and read about love, so we must believe love is real. It exists, and we want it, but do we realize it's a gift we freely have available to us from our Father, and it *is* all we need?

There have been times when believing God's unconditional love is enough was not enough for me. I didn't intentionally declare this fact, but my actions made it clear in hindsight. I was a fool for not realizing it. I've been hurt by worldly love more than once; alas, the expression "fool me once, shame on you; fool me twice, shame on me." I kept getting disappointed until I realized there was a love that wouldn't disappoint: God's love. His is unconditional, everlasting, and what I wanted all along. I'm compelled to believe we are afraid to trust love for a variety of reasons, or we perhaps don't understand love. Why can't we always take love at face value?

When loving others, depending on how we look at love, it may be challenging for us if we don't understand the other person's true feelings. Emotions are many times misunderstood or misinterpreted. *The Five Love Languages* by Dr. Gary Chapman is a wonderful book that helps highlight each of our different natures to show and receive love. For example, I feel loved by spending quality time with people I care about. They don't all require that same quality time to know I love them, so they may not pursue quality time with me the way I pursue quality time. Fortunately, my people all "get me" as I do them, so this isn't an issue for us. It's helpful that I recognize this and know their love languages so that I'm not disappointed by expectations.

Love is active, meaning it grows, shifts, and evolves. Exploring how we can love others where they are emotionally and based on their particular love language is far less frustrating than simply showering people with love we think they want. In essence, that can burden the one receiving the love by feeling pressured to reciprocate in ways that aren't natural for them.

The five Love Languages are acts of service, giving gifts, words of affirmation, physical touch, and my primary love language, quality time. Honing in on one another's love language is an incredible tool available for developing insight for successful, loving relationships. I believe we carry this wisdom into all relationships, including those with our neighbor. We have an opportunity to fine-tune our perspectives for authenticity and potentially foster growth, healing, and even forgiveness in strained relationships.

As much as I want to give myself a high score for healthy relationships in loving God and my neighbor, there's definitely room for improvement. I've recently asked myself, "What kind of friend do I make? Am I a good neighbor? God is asking this of me, so what grade would I issue myself? If I read about someone in distress, is my response to pray or to reach out? How do I justify my decisions to either engage or stay silent? What about my literal neighbors? Do I know how they are doing?" This lightning round of questioning is a good exercise for introspection. Keep your answers to yourself. (Or share them with your neighbor.)

When I was growing up, our family knew every neighbor on our street. We knew where they were from, what they did for a living, and their hobbies and interests. One neighbor had us over to play her piano and listen to patriotic tunes; another neighbor let us rake all the leaves in their yard each fall to create a giant leaf pile for jumping. One neighbor allowed all the kids to come swim in their pool, and another offered their field for kickball.

My mom was the neighbor who baked homemade gingerbread men for Halloween treats, and a few doors away was the lady who always offered a friendly smile when we were selling candy for the school fundraiser. I can say with confidence that I liked all our neighbors from those days and reflect with fondness on how we all were there for our families in good times and difficult times.

Not everyone had this same experience, and I'm not suggesting that you have to go on a crusade to know your literal neighbor today. That can look like pressure, which isn't my intent. I do believe we have an opportunity, the option really, to notice those in our sphere: the people we cross paths with, from the workplace to those in the grocery checkout line to our logistical neighbor. The world looked a lot different when I was growing up in that we didn't have any digital presence to broaden our world. By default, it seemed more closely knit, but even then not everyone shared my idyllic view. This could make it difficult to feel love for our neighbor, as we're called to do.

Loving our neighbors, literal or not, can simply mean taking the time to notice their needs and offer a hand. Like the Good Samaritan who noticed and came to the aid of the man beaten by robbers, we are called to love those different from us and to love in all circumstances. Our neighbors are all God's people. I can remember hearing the Good Samaritan story as a little girl in Sunday school and for many years after. I got the premise, but what I didn't consider for a long time was the depth of what it truly means to love my neighbor. The Samaritan showed kindness to his neighbor who would ordinarily rebuke him and be disgusted by him. Now I have to ask, do I love like the Samaritan?

> But he, desiring to justify himself, said to Jesus, "And who is my neighbor?" Jesus replied, "A man was going down from Jerusalem to Jericho, and

he fell among robbers, who stripped him and beat him and departed, leaving him half dead. Now by chance a priest was going down that road, and when he saw him he passed by on the other side. So likewise a Levite, when he came to the place and saw him, passed by on the other side. But a Samaritan, as he journeyed, came to where he was, and when he saw him, he had compassion. He went to him and bound up his wounds, pouring on oil and wine. Then he set him on his own animal and brought him to an inn and took care of him." (Luke 10:29–34)

If we're going to love our neighbor as God asks, that means we need to have compassion for them, pray for them, and, yes, forgive them as well as ask forgiveness from them. Forgiveness can be a touchy subject. It can be met with major resistance, and although there may be valid reasons to feel resistance, that doesn't make it all right not to forgive. Time does heal, it's true, but God asks us to forgive our brothers and sisters as He has forgiven us. I don't know if there's an expectation of how soon we need to forgive someone who's hurt us, but I know He is asking us to forgive, so what are we waiting for? Maybe we're too bruised, maybe it's our pride, or maybe we're afraid to forgive. Forgiveness can offer permission to be hurt again, and we aren't necessarily up for that at all.

It's also possible we're the one needing forgiveness. It can be a crippling emotion of guilt and shame if we are knowingly aware of our offense. Pesky pride might help us fend off the immediate need to ask for forgiveness, but ultimately, forgiving each other is what we're called to do in order to fully love. I've experienced all of the excuses, pride, shame, guilt, hurt, and fear. It's especially difficult to forgive one another when we have our hearts at stake, and I'm certain that the level of the offense has determined the speed of forgiveness. "Be kind to one another, tenderhearted, forgiving one another, as God in Christ forgave you" (Ephesians 4:32).

"To err is human, to forgive is divine." This notable quote from Alexander Pope, an English poet in 1711, spoke on what it means to be a Christian. He acknowledged how we make mistakes but should strive to be more like God and forgive others, not criticize so much. How many times have you heard the expression, "I can forgive, but I won't ever forget"? What does this even mean? Is this really forgiveness? Walker would say no, it's not. In fact, he would say you're either all in or not. His exact words were "Don't half-'bleep' it." Either you forgive fully, or you're not actually forgiving but acting to possibly manipulate in your head or heart that you've forgiven.

The mistake can be made that forgiveness is what we're giving to someone who's hurt us. That's a lie. The person we struggle to forgive doesn't necessarily know how we feel, so while they're oblivious to our feelings, we're carrying this weight on our shoulders of our grievance against our loved one, our neighbor. If we ask whether pain from the hurt is still serving us like a self-inflicted wound, we may discover we don't want to heal. It will take work in some instances, just as when we're on crutches from a broken bone; time will heal the bone, and we'll no longer need to rely on the crutches. We actually have a choice, and the truth is that forgiveness frees us from what has kept us from a closer relationship not only with our neighbor but also with God.

We may not feel like forgiving, but as I've already said, God is asking us to forgive so nothing keeps our hearts hostage or keeps us from truly loving our neighbor. There may be times we feel we don't deserve forgiveness or the other person doesn't deserve it, but do any of us really deserve it? Christ died so all our sins would be forgiven, past, present, and future. Knowing this, we can humbly ask for God's continued grace and grant the same grace to our neighbor as we would like that grace bestowed on us. "The whole law is fulfilled in one word: 'You shall love your neighbor as yourself'" (Galatians 5:14).

I would give myself a decent grade on the subject of forgiveness, but in other areas of loving my neighbor, I'm still a work in progress. Reconciling my own sin nature isn't an attractive exercise, but it's necessary for my growth to love more like Jesus. On occasion I can be selfish, judgmental, prideful, haughty, and even *covetous*. I've actually been excited to introduce the tenth Commandment, as it packs a punch and shouldn't be underestimated.

Although God saved coveting for last, I doubt it was meant for less importance. We, however, often treat it as less important than all of His other commandments. Examining my heart, I'm aware I once grappled with coveting in prior seasons of my life, but at the time, I didn't realize it. How I didn't grasp what I was doing is a little embarrassing to admit. Coveting my neighbor's "donkey" in effect made me less loving of my neighbor. Exodus 20:17 says, "You shall not covet your neighbor's house; you shall not covet your neighbor's wife, or his male servant, or his female servant, or his ox, or his donkey, or anything that is your neighbor's." I never wanted to take or steal from my neighbor, then or now; I simply may have wanted what they have for myself as well. In my case, it's not an actual donkey that I've coveted, but I have coveted my neighbor's house, address, lifestyle, purse, car, and relationships.

I don't struggle with coveting nearly as much anymore. I like to rest in the awareness that I've grown not to covet because I've gained contentment with what I have been given. This has taken years of growth, and although at times I catch myself longing for this or that, I quickly come back to my reality with gratitude.

There was a time years ago when the home I had wasn't enough for me. I wanted bigger, more beautiful, a better location, more bells and whistles, and a more desirable address. I didn't tell anyone about my desires because I was a little embarrassed to have these wishes—especially since my home was in a lovely and "coveted" neighborhood. Here's the crazy thing about coveting: it's the only commandment that you break with your thoughts, not your actions. God knew my thoughts then, and He knows ours today, so it's not harmless if we just think about our desires. It's still sin!

To covet is to wish, crave, or long for something of someone else's. When we want our neighbor's possessions for our own, it may seem harmless to wish we could have what they have, but the danger in doing this is (a) we're sinning, which drives us apart from loving our neighbors and God, but (b) we're not fully loving God because we're not acknowledging our abundance from Him. If we examine our individual abundance, it will look different for each of us, but it's abundance. Think about it; we have so much more than we deserve. I've heard countless stories of God-fearing people who seemingly have nothing in tangible possessions yet are joyous, living a rich life. This abundance is relevant to the beholder and a lesson to be learned.

Abundance became very clear to me on my fiftieth birthday. It was by far one of the highlights of my life. My husband and I spent a few days before Christmas with my family, including my children, mom, and stepdad, my brother and sister-in-law, my nephews, and my dear friends Mary Neal and Keith. Everyone traveled to meet in the Texas hill country surrounded by country roads and God's creations. It was then that I professed gratitude of my abundant life to my family. It was incredible! I felt my cup overflow, realizing all God had given to me, and being with all of my loved ones was the exclamation point. The people I loved most were with me, celebrating my life, sharing stories, and making more memories. This precious gift from all of them couldn't be topped, and it was a turning point for me. I knew no tangible desire could ever bring me a greater reward than time spent with my people. I knew then that I had achieved abundance, and it wasn't in possessions or money. It was abundance in love. It became clear He had delivered this gift to me in more ways than I deserved, and I coveted nothing.

When given the choice to covet from my neighbor or bask in gratitude, the latter is what fulfills me. It would be so easy to covet a different life or circumstance when met with roadblocks in our lives. But being reminded of His provisions needs to be enough. I encourage everyone to seek this place of peace versus coveting what will likely result in a dead end spiritually. He has always provided and always will provide for us. This doesn't mean being spared trials and suffering. Without a doubt one of the most painful periods of my life has been in recent years. But knowing God had my back and would provide for me is how I managed to forge onward and grow even closer in a deeper relationship with God. It was actually when I fell head over heels in love with Him. The beauty of this relationship is what we can hope for by following the commandments. It's also our opportunity to help our neighbors navigate into a loving relationship with our Father and with one another.

We may find ourselves the subject of our neighbors' coveting. If we've desired what our neighbor has, isn't it possible our neighbor has had desires for what's ours? We may be used to influence their lives away from their unhealthy desires to the desire God's will intends. Being observant of the world around us for the right reasons will yield positives, so I would say it's how and why we look for perspective that's instrumental for our development. If our eyes are in someone else's lane, going unchecked, coveting can be a gateway to other sins. It's a dangerous risk our hearts may not be positioned to battle and can manifest into other sins.

In old Western movies, the bad guys would ride into an innocent town, scaring townspeople. Outlaws would steal a man's horse and maybe his gal for sport and even shoot a bystander. This is clearly my imagination run amuck, but in our lives today we see similar stories play out all too often in the news. For various reasons, people will see something they want and take it. Whether they feel entitled or desperate, they had to think about it first, covet it. It could be a car, jewelry, a person, or a fill-in-the-blank possession, but to covet, to have a thought to want something that isn't ours, has to come before any action. The enemy will lie to us, and if we aren't careful, we will find ourselves believing the lies that we deserve the thing or are entitled to it—that is, justification. *This* is the disconnect we experience and why caution is recommended about this sleeper Commandment. In essence, coveting highlights our discontentment, which takes our focus away from gratitude.

> "The thief comes only to steal and kill and destroy. I came that they may have life and have it abundantly" (John 10:10).

The key to conquering any sin is putting our thoughts toward our loving heavenly Father first; then all will fall into place. If coveting, divert to following His Commandments: "I am the Lord thy God …. You shall have no other gods before me" (Exodus 20:2–3). We can't allow what isn't already satisfying us to become our idol, desire, or focus more than God. The more I have delved into the commandments, the clearer it is that no matter what my temporary discontentment may be, once I pray about it, seek God in my weakness, and ask forgiveness, He helps me recognize my already joyful and joy-filled life.

To have a joyful and joy-filled life, loving God as we're called to do will find us here. Because He loves us, are we to simply trust this truth and love Him right back? Yes! The Bible tells us so, specifically. "And he said to him, 'You shall love the Lord your God with all your heart and with all your soul and with all your mind'" (Matthew 22:37). I believe when we start loving Him, we will realize how much He already loves us! Before we repent and ask for Him to be our Savior, He's already loved us. He's asking us to love Him too.

If this is all truth, as I believe it is, and we are forgiven of our sins, some may ask why we still need the Ten Commandments.

> So the law is holy, and the commandment is holy
> and righteous and good. (Romans 7:12)

> Do not think that I have come to abolish the Law
> or the Prophets; I have not come to abolish them
> but to fulfill them. (Matthew 5:17)

I believe they are still quite relevant, and it's big deal to continuing following them. Since there's freedom in asking His forgiveness of our sins, what are we asking forgiveness for without the Ten Commandments? This is my rational argument. It's wise and good to ask for His forgiveness of our new sin, confess, and repent, showing awareness or the conscientiousness to change. I don't believe we have to ask for forgiveness over and over to go to heaven, but I do believe if we are to be in a fully loving relationship with God, we need to acknowledge our sins to God.

In my mid twenties I can remember confessing to my mom a deep secret pain I had experienced years before. She had no idea of my suffering and was saddened that I hadn't felt I could confide in her at the time I was hurting. I recall being afraid she wouldn't react the way I needed her to for me to feel supported. It's odd because my mom and I have always been close, but in this case, I may not have told her because I was ashamed. In other words, I didn't seek the unconditional love of my mom when I really needed her love and support the most because of my shame and fear. I made that decision for her, and I deprived her of covering me in her abundant love. Truthfully, I hurt my mom by keeping her at arm's distance in this situation. Our relationship wasn't fully honest because I had kept a part of me from her that she deserved to know. She wasn't angry with me, but she was sad that I didn't believe I could trust her in my time of need. Her joy as a parent is to be there when I need her and to help me navigate the rough waters. This is how I see God. I believe He wants us to turn to Him in all circumstances and be honest with Him in all circumstances.

From that moment, I learned it wasn't up to me to make decisions for someone else. I robbed us both of a precious time for her to parent and for me to receive what I longed for—to feel loved and safe. I believe this is how we treat God sometimes. We attempt to hide our pains from Him and trick ourselves into believing He can't see our shame. The fallacy is that He already knows our sins and what we long to feel. Our parents will forgive us unconditionally, as my mom has time and again. At the same time, a strong and trusting relationship can't be realized until there's restoration. We get that through confession and asking forgiveness. Although all our sins were forgiven at the cross, we still need to confess them to our heavenly Father, not to make sure our salvation is still secure, but as an acknowledgement of what Jesus did for us. It's about strengthening our relationship with God and removing any barriers in our relationship with Him.

If we walk in the light, as he is in the light, we
have fellowship with one another, and the blood of
Jesus his Son cleanses us from all sin. (1 John 1:7)

Understanding, receiving, and showing love with God and
our neighbors can at times be challenging to take at face value
for a myriad of reasons. Love heals, love binds, love inspires, but
love can also hurt. Hearts have broken, and lives have been deeply
shattered by love. The blessing of discovering the difference in
knowing God's love is that He never leaves us, always loves us, and
won't ever hurt us! In certain circumstances in this broken and
sin-filled world, it may feel as if God has hurt us by allowing hurt
to happen. In these moments we may not understand the why,
but we can shift to asking God what to do in the circumstance.
And we can ask Him to be present with us while we're in it. God
doesn't create pain; He is the Healer in the hurt.

My daily ambition is to go to Him, talk with Him, lean on
Him, listen to Him, depend on Him, trust Him, include Him in
my life completely, and love Him with all my heart, all my soul,
and all my mind. This is how a loving relationship works in my
opinion. If we can simplify our understanding of these truths and
accept His love as a free gift available to us all, our willingness
to love Him back will manifest in beautiful ways, including how
we love others.

There's a popular Christian folk song written in 1966 by a
former catholic priest, Peter Raymond Scholtes, called "They will
know we are Christians by our love." It's also known as "One in
the Spirit." The lyrics are a direct interpretation of God's breathed
Word: "By this all people will know that you are my disciples, if
you have love for one another" (John 13:35). I've always loved this
song and can remember singing it in youth group many times.
Over the years many artists have sung this wonderful song, and

each time I hear it, I feel grounded in the clear truth that we are indeed one in the Spirit and one in the Lord. These truths reflect love.

Most of us love a love story. I become almost giddy when receiving a love letter or love note from Curt. We each have access to the ultimate Love Letter written to us every day from our Father in the Bible. My husband says the Bible reads as God's love story to us. God has so lovingly shown us how to love. Our opportunity now lies in the freedom to walk lovingly with the Lord and our neighbors side by side. In doing so, we will have our own love stories to sing about, write about, and shout about from mountaintops. To quote again the song title, "They will know we are Christians by our love."

WHAT ARE YOUR THOUGHTS?

1) Have you ever written or received a love letter? How did that feel? If you wrote a love letter to God, how would you begin the letter?

_____

_____

_____

_____

2) What's your love language? How can you use it to love your neighbor?

_____

_____

_____

3) Do you struggle with forgiveness? Is there someone you need to ask to forgive you? Or someone you "say" you have forgiven, but you have not?

_____

_____

_____

_____

4) Do you recall an instance when coveting distracted you from gratitude for your own abundance?

_____

_____

_____

_____

> Let love be genuine. Abhor what is evil; hold fast to what is good. Love one another with brotherly affection. Outdo one another in showing honor. Do not be slothful in zeal, be fervent in spirit, serve the Lord. Rejoice in hope, be patient in tribulation, be constant in prayer. Contribute to the needs of the saints and seek to show hospitality.
>
> Bless those who persecute you; bless and do not curse them. Rejoice with those who rejoice, weep with those who weep. Live in harmony with one another. Do not be haughty, but associate with the lowly. Never be wise in your own sight. Repay no one evil for evil, but give thought to do what is honorable in the sight of all. If possible, so far as it depends on you, live peaceably with all. (Romans 12:9–18)

SUMMING IT UP ...

Whatever was written in former days was written for our instruction, that through endurance and through the encouragement of the Scriptures we might have hope. May the God of endurance and encouragement grant you to live in such harmony with one another, in accord with Christ Jesus, that together you may with one voice glorify the God and Father of our Lord Jesus Christ. Therefore welcome one another as Christ has welcomed you, for the glory of God.

—Romans 15:4–7

Thank you for taking the journey with me on the winding road through the Ten Commandments. I hope that you've enjoyed the experience! I wrote about His commandments in this way because God led me to for His purposes—not just for me, but also for you. I believe it was important to walk through each Commandment personally to better understand a variety of perspectives. No matter where you are on your journey with God, after reading *Commanding Reverence*, I pray you too have found new perspectives of their relevance and reverence in your life and in our modern world. I also pray you've grown in your faith, grown in your relationship with God, and grown in how you love others.

We have one God, and He unconditionally loves. He forgives, He shows us grace and mercy, He wants us to be joyful, joy-filled, and to know the peace and contentment that come with abiding in Him and loving Him. My intent in writing this book was for you to consider the Ten Commandments from a heart view, not as a rulebook. If we have a transformation of our hearts, we will build a closer relationship with Christ and recognize that His "guardrails" were given to us because He loves us. If we don't regard the Ten Commandments as necessary for our abundance, God loves us anyway. If we don't, our salvation is still secure. If we don't, we still can have a relationship with Him, but it likely won't be in its richest blend. It's like having a family dinner without the head of the family being included. God wants to be invited into our hearts and our daily lives. It's up to us to seek that relationship. He isn't going to force us, because He loves us.

How we start the heart transformation and daily walk of noticing the Ten Commandments is with prayer. He has shown us how to start praying, and I encourage you to ask God to help you begin to recognize the areas in your life that might need awareness of healing and growth. Answer the questions at the end of the each chapter and at the end of the book. Whether you discuss them in a small group, with your spouse or a friend, or on your own, taking time to reflect on these questions will offer a new lens for understanding your need for obedience to His commands. We each have our own unique journey, and it's exciting to know that God is with us along the way.

God gave us the Ten Commandments because He loves us. They provide a framework for us to find true abundance. There's no mystery with the Lord. It's important to ditch our self-righteous checklists, not cherry-pick from the "commandment buffet" and be cautious to risk not receiving all the benefits of fulfilling relationships should we discount His Commandments. If we trust God for the wisdom we seek, and put Him before ourselves, then knowing love of our Mighty God will be more wonderful than imagined.

Lastly, we are called to be disciples, so share your wisdom with the people God places in your path. We are all called to grow His kingdom, so meeting our neighbors where they are is critical. He asked me to glorify Him by using my voice in writing this book. Pray over how He has called you to use your gifts for the kingdom, and then take the first steps!

> Go therefore and make disciples of all nations, baptizing them in the name of the Father and of the Son and of the Holy Spirit, teaching them to observe all that I have commanded you. And behold, I am with you always, to the end of the age. (Matthew 28:19–20)

ADVICE FROM MY CHILDREN
AND MENTORS

"Be cautious not to approach the Ten Commandments like a CrossFit class. High-intensity competition with yourself or others isn't the play. Being better at understanding them is great but only if your goal is to consistently grow for the right reasons. This isn't a pass-fail checklist of how we're doing. God gave them to us as a framework to live by. Just like a house needs a strong foundation to build on, so do we." —Dawson

"Look at the Ten Commandments as guideposts holding virtue and values for us to follow. Sustaining man for centuries, clinch their infinite meaning. They are powerful!" —Paul

"Keep it simple! Ask yourself how you're doing in obedience following the Ten Commandments, and adjust as needed. God loves us regardless, but what they say is what they mean. He asks us to follow them, and when you mess up, which you will, ask God to forgive you as an acknowledgement of your mistake, and He will. Remember to be sincere without manipulation in your heart." —Walker

"We could be living more like Him if we follow the Ten Commandments! Aspire to surround yourself with people who strive to seek and live in a relationship with God. Consider that we may be the vessel God uses to bring others closer to Christ. An occasional sermon may be the only avenue to learn messages for some people, so awareness of how we can encourage more opportunities and conversation with our peers is important. We are the disciples God calls to use our voices. Ask Him how He wants you to use your voice for His kingdom." —Ellie

"Keep in mind that God gave them to us for a purpose." —Joye

"Everything we do matters. Being obedient to the Ten Commandments glorifies God, and following them is the roadmap to how we're supposed to treat each other and love God." —Nick

"It's critically important to move from a life of trying to earn our way into heaven by gaining God's approval. We must acknowledge we need a savior, love our neighbor, and love God. Be in relationship with Him, seek Him, and keep being disciples by allowing God to use us. Slow down, stop being so busy, and take care of our natural world. This will allow us to hear how God wants to use us in loving others." —Tim

"Love God more than ourselves; don't look at ourselves as gods. Love Him first. When we trust in the Ten Commandments, we will live a more fulfilling life. There's an urgency; follow them, know them so you can know God." —Jim

"Always remember *whose* you are! It's who you are, what you are, and how you are that shines through and makes you lovely." —my beautiful mom

PERSPECTIVE ...

1) What surprised you most while reading *Commanding Reverence*?

_____

_____

_____

_____

2) How will you use what you've learned to grow in your relationship with Christ and bring others closer to Christ?

_____

_____

_____

_____

3) Describe which Commandment you most misunderstood or misused before reading *Commanding Reverence*.

_____

_____

_____

_____

4) What steps are you going to take in an effort to better follow God's Commandments?

_____

_____

_____

_____

ABOUT THE COVER

Similar to my experience writing the book, the cover design was also a journey. For so long I didn't have a vision, but knew God would provide and He did. I always believed the color blue would be a part of the cover but beyond that, it was unclear for some time.

During quiet reflection while visiting our family home in northern Michigan, it came to me that I was to use one of my late cousin's paintings. My cousin Donna was quite talented and her paintings captured the essence of the area "Up North" I truly love.

Two of Donna's granddaughters, Kit and Evie, talented in their own right, contributed their time and imaginations assisting me in the creative process. This process, lead to Evie producing mock-ups for me to share my vision with the publishing design team. What a special experience for us all!

As clear as knowing the color blue and one of Donna's paintings would be on the cover, it also became clear that the Ten Commandments tablets would be on the cover as well. It took several iterations until I fell upon references of sapphire or lapis tablets as *the chosen stone*, then it all clicked - this was what I had been waiting for and the cover came together.

Until this journey, I hadn't heard the belief by many scholars that the Ten Commandments were written on tablets of sapphire or lapis stone. I had only seen photos and images with them written on gray stone and I believed what I saw to be reality. It seemed logical and not to question until reading from the points of view of those believing they were in fact written by God from gems in heaven.

"...and they saw the God of Israel. There was under his feet as it were a pavement of sapphire stone, like the very heaven for clearness..." (Exodus 24:10)

This scripture describes what the elders witnessed when worshipping on Mount Sinai just two verses before the Ten Commandments were given to Moses.

"The LORD said to Moses, "Come up to me on the mountain and wait there, that I may give you the tablets of stone, with the law and the commandment, which I have written for their instruction." (Exodus 24:12)

Were the tablets God used to write the Ten Commandments carved out of the jeweled pavement in heaven? It can be said that the stones mentioned in the above verse were in reference to the sapphire pavement under God's feet, but whether or not they were in fact used isn't certain.

The color blue is mentioned approximately fifty times in the Bible. In classical Hebrew the word *sapir* can be translated as lapis or *lazuli*, which is a more likely stone to carve versus sapphire because of it's composition. Some sources believe the color blue represents or symbolizes heaven, God, His throne, the Holy Spirit, truth, grace, revelation and the Commandments. Some would say that scripture supports this indication of the commandments on sapphire tablets and it definitely indicates the significance of the color blue relating to the Ten Commandments. A reminder at least -

The LORD said to Moses, "Speak to the people of Israel, and tell them to make tassels on the corners of their garments throughout their generations, and to put a cord of blue on the tassel of each corner. And it shall be a tassel for you to look at and remember all the commandments of the LORD, to do them, not to follow after your own heart and your own eyes, which you are inclined to whore after. (Numbers 15:37-39)

It's not certain on what stone God wrote the Ten Commandments, but I'm intrigued by the possibility of them being written on gems from the pavement under His feet. My perspective - it's a thought worth considering!

PLAYLIST INSPIRING ME ALONG THIS JOURNEY

"Singing to The Lord is Worship! Sing often, Sing out loud and Sing with all your heart!!"

I Can Only Imagine – Mercy Me
Voice of Truth – Casting Crowns
Thy Word – Amy Grant
The Blessing – Kari Jobe & Cody Carnes
Be Alright – Danny Gokey & Evan Craft
We Praise You – Brandon Lake
Gratitude – Brandon Lake
I Got Saved – Selah
Raise a Hallelujah – Bethel Music
Echo Holy – Red Rock Worship
Goodness of God – The Worship Initiative, Bethany Barnard
Isn't He (This Jesus) – The Belonging Co, Natalie Grant
Peace Be Still – The Belonging Co, Lauren Daigle
Who You Say I Am – Hillsong Worship
Come Thou Fount – Chris Tomlin
We Fall Down – Chris Tomlin
Spirit of the Living God – Vertical Worship
Build My Life – Pat Barrett
Getting Started – Jeremy Camp
Battle Belongs – Phil Wickham
Evidence – Josh Baldwin
How Great Thou Art – Carrie Underwood
Holy Spirit Come – Patrick Mayberry
Waymaker – Michael W. Smith
Love God Love People – Danny Gokey

NOTES

CHAPTER ONE: GOD'S GUARDRAILS

1. Rev. George Mastrantonis, *The Ten Commandments,* https://ascensionfairview.org/our-faith/ten-commandments/ *2022*

2. William J. Federer's paper regarding the Ten Commandments and American History in documents updated July 31, 2015 cited on *Godempowersyou.com.* Specifically highlighting the excerpt regarding John Adams and his belief in God and the Ten Commandments.

3. Comparisons and insight of the Ten Commandments from Roman Catholic perspective. Honing in on The Sabbath some historical timelines relating to the Ten Commandments and the Bible. *the-ten-commandments.org/romancatholic-tencommandments.html.* Last modified November 2, 2020.

4. Dutch Sheets, GiveHim15 March 22, 2022, *Pray for Americas Judges.* https://www.givehim15.com/post/march-22-2022.

5. Definition of Confirmation in Episcopal Church, https://*episcopalchurch.org/glossary/confirmation*

6. Administrator, NeverThirsty.org https://www.neverthirsty.org/bible-qa/qa-archives/question/do-we-have-to-keep-the-commandments-and-laws-given-in-the-old-testament/

CHAPTER TWO: MYTHS AND CONSEQUENCES
1. John Calahan, retired pastor author and teaching minister for *Neverthirsty.org.* Entry article in archives *neverthirsty.org/bible-qa/qa-archives/question/can-be-forgiven-taking-gods-name-in-vain/*

2. Dictionary.com article published December 19, 2018 titled *The Surprisingly Religious Background of "Golly," "Gosh," and "Gee."*

3. Bible Translations *https://www.the-ten-commandments.org/ten-commandments-bible-translations.html.*

CHAPTER THREE: SELF RIGHTEOUS CHECKLIST
1. *Judaism: The Ten Commandments* https://jewishvirtuallibrary.org/the-ten-commandments

2. Pew Research Center published article October 17, 2019, In U.S., Decline of Christianity Continues at Rapid Pace.

3. Sarah Mae Saliong, *Only 6% of Americans Believe Biblical Worldveiw, Barna Survey Reveals*, May 27, 2021 https://www.christianitydaily.com/articles/11996/20210527/only6-percent-0f-americans-believe-biblical-worldview-barna-survey-reveals-family-research-council.htm

4. Sarah Mae Saliong, May 4, 2021, *Barna Poll Finds Many Americans Believe In 'Moralistic Therapeutic Deism' —Or Simply Put, 'Feel-Good Fake Christianity,'* https://www.christianitydaily.com/articles/11724/20210504/barna-poll-finds-many-americans-believe-in-moralistic-therapeutic-deism-—or-simply-put-feel-good-fake-christianity.htm

5. Nathaniel Hawthorne, *The Scarlet Letter,* 1950 Random House Publishers, Inc.

6. Austin Cline. *"Comparing the Ten Commandments."* Learn Religions, Jul. 29, 2021, learnreligions.com/different-versions-of-the-ten-commandments-250923.

7. Administrator, Knowing-Jesus.com, *12 Bible Verses about Being Seen By Man*, https://bible.knowing-jesus.com/topics/Being-Seen-By-Man

CHAPTER 4: RELIGIOUS BUFFET

1. Dr. Michael L. Williams, *You Shall Not Bear False Witness: Bible Lesson and Life Application.* https://www.whatchristians wanttoknow.com/you-shall-not-bear-false-witness-bible-lesson-and-life-application

CHAPTER 5: RISKY BUSINESS

1. Scot Longyear, Senior Pastor Maryland Community Church Sermon Series 2021

2. *Episcopal Book of Common Prayer*, Confession of Sin, Prayers of the People Form VI.

3. Ann Voskamp featured guest, *The Happy Hour* podcast with Jamie Ivey, jamieivey.com/HH481.

4. Scott Ramsey, *Light at the End of the Tunnel*, Your Everyday Life Blog, https://youreverdaylife.org/light-at-the-end-of-the-tunnel, April 18, 2022.

5. Gabe Lyons, *The Christian View - What is the full Christian story and how does it affect our witness?* Instagram post July 20, 2021.

CHAPTER SIX: WISE OWLS

1. Erwin, *Why are owls considered wise?* September 17, 2013, https://www.knowswhy.com/why-are-owls-wise/

2. General Administrator, *Are we too hard on our children (and ourselves) for disrespecting elders?* January 3, 2018, https://www.my-emotions.in/blog/children-disrepsect

CHAPTER SEVEN: WHAT WE WORSHIP

1. Don Ruhl, Savage Street Church of Christ, Oregon, *Sevens in the Bible,* last updated June 23, 2022, https://sevensinthebible.com/list-of-sevens-in-the-bible/.

2. Jesse Oakley, Your Tango. *What Does The Number 7 Mean In The Bible & Numerology,* August, 3, 2019. https://www.yourtango.com/2019326062/meaning-number-7-according-bible-numerology.

3. Angel Number Copyright 2022, *What Does the Number 7 Mean in the Bible and Prophetically,* https://angelnumber.org/what-does-the-number-7-mean-in-the-bible/

4. Dutch Sheets, *Exposing the Source of Evil in America,* giveHim15, July 23, 2021. https://www.givehim15.com/post/july-23-2021(Givehim15 on YouTube, July 23, 2021)

5. Ben Davis, February 3, 2019, *Why is 7 a lucky number in the Bible?* https://www.mvorganizing.org/why-is-7-a-lucky-number-in-the-bible/

6. Matthew Ervin, March 7, 2014, Apple Eye Ministries. *The Seven Feast of Israel are Fulfilled in Jesus,* http://appleeye.org/2014/03/07/the-seven-feasts-of-israel-are-fulfilled-in-jesus/

7. Becky Little, Last Updated March 29, 2021, History.com, How the Seven Deadly Sins Began as 'Eight Evil thoughts', https://www.history.com/news/seven-deadly-sins-origins

8. Father David Meconi, February 1, 2020, Catholic.com, *The Seven Deadly Sins and how to overcome them in your life*, https://www.catholic.com/magazine/print-edition/the-seven-deadly-sins

9. Administrator, Got Questions Ministries, last updated January 4, 2022, *Is God opposed to pleasure?* https://www.gotquestions.org/God-pleasure.html

CHAPTER EIGHT: LOVE

1. Hasa, Pediaa.com, May 13, 2020, *Difference Between Envy and Covet.* https://pediaa.com/difference-between-envy-and-covet/

2. Johsua Taylor, Discipleship Ministries, June 26, 2019. *History of Hymns: 'They'll Know We Are Christians by Our Love'* https://www.umcdiscipleship.org/articles/history-of-hymns-theyll-know-we-are-christians-by-our-love

3. Danielle Burnock, Crosswalk.com contributing writer, Christianity.com, May 14, 2020. *Do Christians Have to Keep Asking for Forgiveness for Their Sins?* https://www.christianity.com/wiki/salvation/do-christians-have-to-keep-asking-for-forgiveness-for-their-sins.html

REFERENCED THROUGHOUT

Sara Louisas, The Salt of the Earth. *The Commandments of God and the Commandments of Jesus Christ,* https://www.the-saltoftheearth.com/the-commandments-of-god-and-the-commandments-of-jesus/

ABOUT THE COVER

1. Matthew Ervin, Apple Eye Ministries, June 15, 2014. *The Ten Commandments were Written on Sapphire Tablets From God's Throne.* http://appleeye.org/2014/06/15/the-ten-commandments-were-written-on-sapphire-tablets-from-gods-throne/

2. Johnny McAwley, SlightlyBlue.com, *Significance of the color Blue in the Bible.* https://slightlyblue.com/culture/blue-in-bible/

3. David Valentine, *The Tablets*, 2019. https://blueten commandments.com/index.html

4. Sue Nelson, Women of Noble Character, *Colors in the Bible Rich with Meaning.* https://www.womanofnoblecharacter.com/blue-in-the-bible/